The Three Pillars of Judaism

The Three Pillars of Judaism

A Search for Faith and Values

Jonathan Wittenberg

SCM PRESS LTD

Copyright © Jonathan Wittenberg 1996

0 334 02665 2

First published 1996 by
SCM Press Ltd
9–17 St Albans Place, London N1 0NX

Typeset at Regent Typesetting, London

Printed in Great Britain by
Biddles Ltd, Guildford and King's Lynn

To all my family,
most especially to Mossy and Libby
who carry our love and hope forward

I would like to thank my wife Nicky, my parents and my friends, especially Gerald and Bettie Rabie and John Schlapobersky, whose suggestions, comments and criticisms have inspired, enriched and improved all that follows. I would particularly like to thank my teachers, Rabbi Dr Magonet for encouraging and helping me to write this book, and Rabbi Dr Louis Jacobs, Rabbi Dr John Rayner, Dr Joanna Weinberg and Rabbi Isaac Levy for their kind and astute support.

Jonathan Wittenberg

Elul 5756, August 1996

Simon the Just was one of the last survivors of the Great Synagogue. He used to say: 'Upon three things the world stands, upon the Torah, upon the Divine Service and upon acts of faithful love' (Chapters of the Fathers 1.2).

Contents

Contents

Introduction

Faith is a response of the whole person to the whole of life. It expresses the commitment to a bond with God both because of, and in spite of, all that our years may bring. Thus a life of faith includes moments of quiet intuition, of confident closeness and of intense awareness of a dimension beyond ourselves, as well as times of doubt, distance, disenchantment, anger and redis-covery. Like our experience of other important relationships, faith is therefore characterized by changes, developments and mood. To define faith in terms of rigid mental positions and dogmatic assertions is to limit and distort it. For faith requires not inner inflexibility but inner persistence, and strength of faith lies in having the courage not only to carry on in spite of, but also to develop because of, the many changes in fortune and feeling that a human lifetime inevitably brings.

A thousand sacred verses speak of God, but it is most of all the testament of the living moment which communicates God's presence. A rabbi, like ministers of all religions, has the privilege of sharing countless moments, small and unpretentious, yet hinting at such presence, with people of every age and stage of life. One learns to try to listen. Elijah experienced the closeness of God in the voice of fine silence that moved him to cover his face with his mantle. Similarly, in little ways, one senses that this same voice still speaks in life, intuited differently by each person and expressed in feelings and responses that are mostly beyond the powers of conscious articulation.

Any statement of theology carries the risk of betraying God by narrowing divinity down to a formula, and of betraying

I

humanity by excluding the valid experiences of different people. Therefore, in an age in which more and more groups seem to be demanding the satisfaction of clear and simple certainties, we should treat the growing cult of the creed with suspicion. I am often reminded of E. M. Forster's comment that he does not believe in belief, holding it to be a kind of starch, a sort of mental stiffening process.[1] If that is what belief really were, rather than a reflection of how it is often presented, I would have to agree with him. But faith is not an intellectual credo, a series of dogmatic propositions which the mind must uphold at all times. Nor is it simply 'one of the secrets of the heart', a thing one either does or does not have, and about which we can do little. Faith is engagement in our relationship with God.

How that process begins must vary. We may be stirred in the course of our life by an intuition, by a sense experienced in a place of worship, or amidst wild nature, or in close conversation with a friend, that there is indeed a further dimension to our existence. We may pursue the matter no further. Or we may be moved to seek ways of discovering more, of drawing closer to the experience that has moved us. Eventually this quest may become the driving force and disciplining principle of our existence; we find ourselves unable to let go of it. For once experienced, the life of the spirit is not easily forgotten; should it wane, the soul mourns until it is vital again.

Thus faith is rooted in experience. It cannot be manufactured; it must be discovered. But, as in every other field of endeavour, what we find will depend on how hard we seek, on the depth and care with which we search. It is this process of searching that I want to write about in the pages which follow. The quest is structured according to the famous saying by Shimeon ha-Tzaddik, Simon the Just, in The Chapters of the Fathers (1.2) that the world stands upon three things, upon Torah, upon the Divine service and upon acts of faithful love. He lived between the third and second centuries BCE but his words define the life of the traditional Jew now as they did then. In considering the subjects to which he refers the recurring question will be how a commitment to prayer, learning and action can extend our spiritual and moral sensitivity and thus bring us closer to God.

A section of the book has been devoted to each of the three areas indicated in Simon the Just's saying (though not in the order in which he places them). The chapter on prayer opens with a comparison between the views of two of the great masters of our century, Abraham Isaac Ha-Cohen Kook and Abraham Joshua Heschel. An analysis of the differences between them leads into a discussion of some of the dilemmas, personal and theological, with which the subject of prayer presents us. Some of the most familiar Jewish prayers are formulated in the language of petition, as if the central object were to ask God for things. Yet we all know that there are times when many blessings, including health, food and freedom from war, are not to be had for all the beseeching in the world. Nevertheless many of us continue to pray, recognizing that it is a basic human need to do so. For prayer is concerned with a central relationship in our lives; it is, depending on how broadly we define it, the principal means we have of addressing ourselves to God. Its value cannot be measured in terms of practical results alone.

The section on Torah opens with a consideration of some of the difficulties the study and practice of it raise: What are the goals of learning? Why is it so important? What is it that makes learning not just an intellectual, but, more significantly by far, a spiritual discipline? With regard to practice, why should we keep the commandments? Can we find an approach to the observance of them which is both respectful and committed, yet which leaves room for difficulties and doubts about, and sometimes even for our criticisms of, Judaism's most sacred texts and traditions? How then can we relate to the Torah's claim of absolute authority and its demand for total obedience? What do we mean by the phrase 'Torah from Heaven' with which this authority is generally explained? What is the place in traditional

Jewish life for choice and personal autonomy? Considering all these questions, is there a particular contribution to be made in our time to the understanding of Torah?

The third section deals with action. Judaism requires us to live in the world and to give definite, tangible expression to our learning and beliefs. The theme of the chapter is not, however, what right values are: it would be easy, and dull, to produce a relatively uncontroversial list of virtues and vices. Instead, the focus is on what are the difficulties, personal and social, which make it so hard for us to live in the way we believe to be right. Why are apparently simple acts of compassion, such as being with the sick and lonely, often so difficult for us to manage? What is the role of community in helping us to carry them out and in protecting us from the temptations of wrongdoing? Is community, as is sometimes now claimed, the answer to all ills, or does it too hold dangers and suffer from limitations? If so, what are the disadvantages of community? How, for example, can we avoid the risk of being unconcerned about, or responding negatively towards those who are not part of our particular group? Where do our responsibilities end?

The final chapter is a reflection on some of our unanswerable questions concerning God. Shimeon ha-Tzaddik does not in fact mention God in his famous saying, but perhaps his emphasis on human responsibility is deliberate. What implications does this carry for our relationship with God? Are there some aspects of it that we stress at the expense of others, leading us to have unhelpful or even inappropriate expectations? Do we need to reevaluate the way we think about God and is Simon the Just implicitly indicating this by stressing what we, rather than what God, must do to safeguard the existence of creation? Does God also need us?

Simon the Just's saying focusses attention on the different facets of Judaism, but it also indicates the need for an integrated approach to life. He doesn't divide experience into the spiritual on the one hand and the worldly on the other, but ascribes as

4

much importance to what we do and how we do it as to the more overtly 'religious' aspects of our lives. I have tried to emphasize this in the subtitle 'A Search for Faith and Values'. It is important to stress the need for an active partnership between faith and values. The genuinely religious community neither can nor should live in isolation from the ethical and social dilemmas of the time. There is only limited value in looking inwards if our investigations have no impact on our sense of responsibility when we look outwards again. Judaism has to – and does – tell us something not only about God and the soul, but also about our attitude to cruelty, hunger, racism, transport policy and bio-diversity. It is hard to believe in a God who does not require us to care about such things. At the same time we are weakened if we are concerned only with matters of conscience and policy, but neglect the domain of the spirit. For it is hard to make serious and prolonged commitments to anything worthwhile without having access to the deepest sources of inspiration, replenishment and truth available to the human being. The life of faith facilitates our contact with these resources not simply on a haphazard, but on a regular and disciplined basis. It cannot of course make that contact happen, but it creates the preconditions for a relationship with God that has the power to refine our insight, restore our spirit and strengthen our purpose.

The emphasis is equally on the word *search*. I have a deep distaste for loud expressions of certainty, preferring by far the quieter, less self-assured, language of the seeker. I know that many see in the acknowledgment of doubt and change signs of weakness, but I do not subscribe to this view. The readiness to question one's beliefs and the awareness that they are the product of discovery and tentative reflection prove that they have their source in genuine experience, and that what is said is not a slogan but something actually felt.

I have tried to be honest and open about the difficulties, as well as the privileges, encountered in trying to live and believe as a Jew. People are not well served by the sweeping assertions and dogmatic affirmations that so frequently seem to characterize the language in which belief is described. Such expressions serve mainly to alienate the many people whose experiences are more tentative and who feel as a result excluded from what they then describe as the community of 'the real believers'. On a number of occasions I have heard men and women speak of their sense of treachery because they harboured doubts, could not believe in some of the statements in the prayer book, or felt that they found God more in nature than in the synagogue. This has led me to the conviction that if only it were possible to share our true thoughts, we would find that we have more in common than we imagine. Rather than feeling anxious or inadequate, we would increase our understanding and be better able to draw strength from one another.

We should not, however, be satisfied with a complacent agnosticism. It is not good enough to sit back and say, 'I don't know, but nobody can know, so I've done all I can'. If our relationship with God is serious, then, as in every important relationship, we have to live with and work at it through both the good times and the bad. The reason for acknowledging difficulties is to enable us to understand them so that they cease to be barriers and become part of the challenge of the journey. For it is a journey, often a long and difficult journey. Judaism does not wear its heart on its sleeve; it cannot be reduced to a few ready epigrams, to short and simple truths. It is not simply a doctrine but a way of life; it has to be lived, and lived for a significant length of time, if its inner beauty is to become apparent. This is not because Judaism seeks to hide its truths or to make the paths towards their discovery difficult. The reason is rather that there are some things the beholding and comprehending of which we have to work for; only through the search, the journey, can the eyes and the heart be sensitized and purified. The great teacher Hillel, who lived at approximately the same time as Jesus, was famous for his gentleness and patience. When a man once challenged him to teach him the

Torah, a subject to which Hillel's whole life was devoted, while standing on one leg, he did not dismiss the stranger but offered the answer: 'What is hateful to you do not do to your fellow.' This justly famous sentence is followed by the telling, but less known, sequel: 'The rest is commentary, go and learn.'[2] Religion is not a romance. It is concerned not with truths alone, but with their practical realization. It teaches us how to discover and live by them. What we inherit from our ancestors is a path by which we can try to do that. If we wish to follow it, we have no choice but to make the effort to 'go and learn'. This Hillel well knew, but he also appreciated that such commitment cannot be forced; it has to be engendered.

Motivation comes with a growing sense of the value of the endeavour. It is nourished internally by an appreciation of how much our life can be enriched by our faith. It is nourished from the outside by the example of other people whose spiritual sensitivity and courage may inspire us. I think particularly of those older people whose lives show that the sentence 'God is the strength of my heart' (Psalm 73.26) is to them a simple and significant truth. I therefore trust the way of Judaism, appreciating that though it may often be hard, it will guide us on our journey, replenishing our sense of purpose and educating the heart.

I have learnt a great deal from my congregation. Being a rabbi has given me little cause for cynicism. Certainly, one becomes aware of weaknesses, blind spots and indifference; but one discovers far more about our vulnerability, our need for understanding, our desire to do what is right and our search for values, wisdom and spirituality. Dozens, hundreds of conversations with people of all ages, with boys and girls before their Bar or Bat Mitzvah, parents, the elderly, the dying, whether their death was timely or not, and with their relatives, have served to heighten my respect for the spiritual dimension of human experience and to make me ever more aware of our hunger and nakedness in that aspect of our lives.

But such needs are not readily addressed. They raise issues which fit uneasily with the competence and self-confidence which is, or has been until recently, such a significant part of the contemporary self-image. Sometimes it is only in moments of pain that such subjects can be shared. Sometimes an abrasive defensiveness may conceal a loneliness which one had not suspected. Sometimes too much talk provokes embarrassment and leads to renewed respect for a Judaism which teaches us to get on with life and its duties.

Yet there is also a great thirst for knowledge. We are living in a time of spiritual rediscovery. There is a revival of Jewish learning and observance. There is a strong feeling of group identity. These are no mean matters in a world which so much lacks the warmth and sense of being rooted that a community and its traditions can provide. Nevertheless, they are not enough; on another level we seek for more. What about values, social conscience and spirituality? What does Judaism have to say about these things? Where can we find the yearning for the presence of God and the passionate concern for universal justice of which the prophets speak? These are the question to which we seek a response.

I turn to Simon the Just's saying and to the guidance of the Jewish tradition.

I

Prayer

The Blade of Grass Sings to the River

Even to those as small as me,
One among tens of thousands,
Even to the children of affliction
On the shores of disappointment ...
The river calls in love   (Leah Goldberg)

1. *The ways of two modern masters*

For most of us, praying does not come easily. Unsure perhaps of what it involves, but sensing that something important is expected of us, we often find it hard to pray, and harder still to talk about prayer. This state of affairs often makes us feel awkward and self-conscious about prayer, yet prayer makes most sense when it is a natural part of our lives; the more segregated, the more unnatural, it is, the less rewarding we will find it. Unfortunately the environment in which we live does not help us. Recent history, predominant Western values, and the alienation between synagogue and worshipper have all made their impact. Prayer, though never easy, has often been easier of access. It is hard for many of us today even to know where and how to start.

I wish to begin my exploration of these difficulties by considering what I believe to be a significant difference in the way two of the greatest spiritual leaders of our century, Rabbi Abraham Isaac Ha-Cohen Kook and Rabbi Abraham Joshua Heschel, approach the subject of prayer.

The two Rabbis had in fact much in common. Both of them

9

were heirs to Hasidic tradition; hence for both of them *devekut* – cleaving, closeness to God –was an ultimate ideal. They were both poets by temperament, as the sometimes extravagant lyricism of each of their prose styles reveals. They both believed that the roots of prayer were to be traced to the very nature of being, of which it was the essential expression: 'an absolute need' to Rav Kook, an 'ontological necessity' for Heschel. Nevertheless, in spite of all that they had in common, circumstances led them to make key statements about prayer which were in some senses opposite to one another.

Thus, in the introduction to his Siddur, *Olat Re'iah*, Rav Kook writes as follows:

> Prayer is the ideal of all the worlds. All being longs for the source of its vitality, every plant and every bush, every grain of sand and every clod of earth, everything in which vitality is revealed and everything in which vitality is concealed, all the small things of creation and all the great things, the heavens on high and the holy angels, every particle of all that is and every thing in its entirety, all calls out for, longs for, desires and yearns for the beloved perfection of its living, sacred, pure and mighty source on high. The human being absorbs these longings every hour and every moment and is raised up and exalted by his sacred yearnings. The opportunity for these yearnings for the majesty of God to be revealed is provided by prayer, prayer which generates waves of light, which goes forth in the freedom of its might and by the utterance of its sacred speech into the broad spaces of God. Through prayer the human being raises up the whole of creation, unites all that is, lifts up everything, raises all to the source of blessing and the source of life.[1]

Thus for Rav Kook the human being lives in a world permeated by the presence of God: 'The earth is the Lord's and the fullness thereof' (Psalm 24.1). Such an environment ceaselessly nourishes the soul with the subliminal sense of the unity of all being and the universal desire of all things to return to their place of origin in God. Prayer is the privilege of making articulate and explicit the will of all creation, the longing of the part for the whole, of the separate for the complete. In its effect, though, it achieves far more; for, by serving as a channel of communication, it brings about and makes palpable that union of all being, the intuition of which prompted it in the first place. Thus it 'raises all to the source of blessing and the source of life'. Prayer, ultimately, is the meeting of fullness with fullness.

Heschel saw matters differently: If

> prayer is the expression of the sense of being at home in the universe, then the Psalmist who exclaimed, 'I am a stranger on earth, hide not Thy commandments from me' (119.19), was a person who grievously misunderstood the nature of prayer. Throughout many centuries of Jewish history the true motivation for prayer was not 'the sense of being at home in the universe' but the sense of *not* being at home in the universe. We could not but experience anxiety and spiritual homelessness in the sight of so much suffering and evil, in the countless examples of failure to live up to the will of God. That experience gained in intensity by the soul-stirring awareness that God Himself was not at home in the universe, where His will is defied, where His kingship is denied. The Shechinah is in exile, the world is corrupt, the universe itself is not at home ...
>
> To pray, then, means to bring God back into the world ...[2]

For Heschel, the universe does not nourish the human soul with a sense of fullness and wholeness; on the contrary, to be spiritually sensitive means to be aware of a feeling of estrangement. Nothing is at home any more, neither people nor the world nor even God. The spur to prayer is the painful consciousness of moral and spiritual deficiency. The task of prayer is to put this right, to bring God back: 'For to worship is to expand the presence of God in the world. God is transcendent,

but our worship makes Him immanent.'³ Yet in the meantime
the distance remains, and into it enter the discordant sounds
and painful sights of so much of recent history and contemporary life. Thus, though the ultimate purpose of prayer may
remain the same for Heschel as it was for Rav Kook, and
though Heschel, too, may seek to render the Presence of God in
the world a palpable reality, where one has to start from is for
Heschel a far more lonely and discouraging place.

What led these two men, separated in time by a generation
at most, to perceive the world in such different ways?
Temperament and personality might suffice in accounting for
their varying views, but the answer is perhaps also to be sought,
partially at least, in the history and geography of their lives.

Rav Kook was born into a Rabbinic family in the small town
of Grieve in north-western Russia. He grew up within the four
cubits of Torah, an *Illui*, a genius, from childhood. He studied
at the great Yeshivah of Volozhin under the spiritual guidance
of the Netsiv, Rabbi Naphtali Tzvi Berliner, who would visit the
study halls at midnight and at four in the morning every day to
make sure that the song of the study of Torah had not ceased.
He served as Rabbi in Zoimel and then Boisk before his heart
prompted him to accept the call to Jaffa and thence to Jerusalem
and the Chief Rabbinate of Palestine. There he fostered the
physical and spiritual regeneration of the land he loved. He died
in 1935, when the shadows of Nazism had begun to lengthen
across Europe, but before the darkness had fully set in. Why
should he not perceive the world as brim full of the Divine
vitality and prayer as the ready and natural expression of the
longing of that life for its source?

Heschel was nourished by no less rich a Jewish world. But he
then went to study in Berlin, where he often felt alien, fled to
America, saw the world he had known destroyed in the
Holocaust and, while mourning this, watched a large propor-
tion of the Jews around him assimilate and slip away from
communal religious life. There was simply too much evil, too

much materialism, and too much ignorance of and indifference to traditional values, for him to have the same spiritual confidence in his environment as the earlier leader. Only a person who has had to confront existential loneliness can entitle one of his books *Man Is Not Alone*. Heschel felt surrounded neither by people nor by events nor by a culture which reminded one of the proximity of the Divine spirit. God had been forced to retreat from the world. Something was missing in the state of humanity, and Heschel was simply too great and too courageous a person not to try to set it right.

Thus it is possible that the different approaches to prayer of these two masters are prompted by other differences than those of temperament alone. Living in different times, they responded to a different *Zeitgeist*. An analysis of their conclusions therefore yields broad findings: it points to something we have lost, something we seek to be restored to, and to the challenge we have to confront.

If I were to be asked in which of the two worlds described above I live, my answer would have to be that I spend most of my time in the latter. I believe I speak for many, if not most, Jews living at this time. It is not simply a matter of what has happened since Rav Kook died; it is also a question of how we perceive the world around us from a spiritual point of view. Few of us would wish to dispute the optimism of the earlier master: the most precious moments of our lives are small confirmations of his great intuitions. It is rather that for most of us the river of the Divine vitality flows either far off or very deep down. Only rarely do we hear it, if at all. More often than not, we have to take its existence on trust, and the variety and volume of the sounds which drown its murmur out are such that this trust is increasingly difficult to find. In some realm of being life surely seeks its source as it has always done and the – often secret – nourishment of the spirit never ceases. But its influence is nothing like as obvious as the loud and violent impact of modern existence which most of us today absorb from every side. How, then, can we sustain an inner life which, as Rav Kook describes it, pours itself forth naturally in prayer. Many of us, if asked what spiritual life we are aware of both within and around us, would probably answer with some sadness: 'Not enough'. 'Occasional intuitions', we might say, or even 'nothing, apart from memories, needs and hopes'. Emptiness is what many of us often have to begin with. Heschel describes God as in retreat; God is transcendent, waiting for us to make Him immanent. But He may well have to wait a long time. For a God in heaven, however omnipotent, has to be sensed inside us to make us want to pray. By Heschel's analysis, we need the results of prayer to enable us to begin. The difficulty, the challenge, is that often we don't know how to start; we lack not only the fullness but also the confidence necessary to enable us to begin.

Nevertheless, I think that many of us, more perhaps than would openly admit it, believe in the river. We trust those people who have heard it call. Occasionally we are aware that, even if from afar, we are hearing it ourselves. In the imagery of Leah Goldberg's poem, quoted above, we may frequently be on the shores of disappointment, but they are still shores. That, however, is not where we wish to remain. We want to hear the river again, and again and again: it is not enough to know that it flows unless we can also feel it flow.

In some part of ourselves we know that our true home is by that river.

2. *What are we praying for?*

One of the most important tasks which lies before the contemporary community, and most especially before its leaders and teachers, is to redeem the role of prayer. For prayer has the power to bring us and the river closer, to draw God into our lives, but only if we engage in it with humility and in an appropriate manner. We therefore have to begin by asking what prayer is really for. If we expect the wrong things from it, we are almost certain to be disappointed. Often, prayer remains peripheral to our lives because we want it to answer the wrong questions. When the enterprise then fails, as, measured according to such expectations, fail it well may, not only prayer, but religion and God, are experienced as letting us down. How many of us have said, or listened to others say: 'I asked but I was not answered, I called but no reply came.'

Often we expect both too much and too little from prayer. We expect too much in that we want prayer to bring relief for our immediate needs. We expect too little because we seek God's intervention, but we do not necessarily seek God. Consider the explanations which Harold Kushner has heard given for the failure of petitionary prayer. The following list is based on the best part of a lifetime of listening to peoples' sorrows by a sympathetic Rabbi who has himself experienced tragedy:

– You didn't get what you prayed for, because you didn't deserve it.
– You didn't get what you prayed for, because you didn't pray hard enough.
– You didn't get what you prayed for, because God knows what is best for you better than you know.
– You didn't get what you prayed for, because someone else's prayer for the opposite result was more worthy.
– You didn't get what you prayed for, because prayer is a sham, God doesn't hear prayers.
– You didn't get what you prayed for because there is no God.[4]

As Kushner demonstrates, analysis shows none of these responses to be satisfactory. In each case there is simply too much to be explained away; surely all Rabbis have listened at some time or another to the following comments, made out of genuine and immediate pain:

Did my relative not deserve to live as much as so-and-so's who was cured?

Why does God listen to that hypocrite who lives such a selfish life, when others who are kind and helpful every day are ignored?

You say that God acts for the best, but was it really better for my friend that he died, leaving a young widow with three small children?

The theme is familiar, and one could carry on *ad infinitum*. Instead, observes Kushner, the real problem must lie in the other part of the sentence, in the words 'get what you prayed for': it is not the results of the prayer but its purpose that we have to reconsider. What is it that we seek to get? What actually are we praying for?

Part of the difficulty is that we are often taught to think of prayer as essentially about asking for things from God. This approach appears to be warranted not only by the fact that many of our key prayers emphasize this aspect of our relationship to God, but also by the manner in which God is presented in much of the Siddur, the daily prayer book, ever familiar but ever challenging. God is the All-Knowing, All-Powerful and All-Providing. Whatever is wrong, surely God can make it better; when we ask, why should God not answer? Any criticism of such an approach must, however, be one of degree only; it would be quite wrong to imply that Judaism in any way rejects the idea of petitionary prayer. On the contrary, as has already been indicated, such a key part of the liturgy as the Amidah, which is said three times daily, is largely composed of requests to God. But the concept of petitionary prayer has nevertheless always been problematic. The Rabbis of the Talmud stressed the importance of the use of the plural; the individual petitioner was to include his or her specific request in a prayer for the general needs of the community. That emphasis is reflected to this day in the wording of the Amidah in which we say: grant *us* healing, bless *our* year, hear *our* prayer, rather than grant *me* or even forgive *me*. In this way personal supplication was broadened into a request on behalf of all people. The fulfilment of one's prayers was therefore realized, not in some private turn of fortunes but in the betterment of society as a whole, a goal for which we were thereby reminded to work harder.

But this was scarcely to be considered a sufficient solution. For some of the Hasidic teachers it didn't go far enough. Could it really be the case, they argued, that we turn to God for the mere purpose of having our mundane needs met? Petitionary prayer could be justified only on the grounds that it was God's, not our own, needs that we were praying for. A deficiency in the world represented, as it were, a lack in the indwelling aspect of the Divine Presence that suffered with us in all our varied fortunes. Thus we were to pray for the sake of God, not merely for ourselves. But this interpretation remained open to the criticism of being no more than theological juggling: it was all too easy to see one's own need as God's need without necessarily enlarging one's horizons or deepening one's sense of the presence of the Divine in the world.

A modern approach has been to see the purpose of petitionary prayer as a way of redirecting our attention to our own responsibilities towards society. Lionel Blue expresses this with customary wit:

> Prayers can act like boomerangs. We get incensed by this or that, and indignantly ask God to do something about it, to take a hand in it as it were. But God is spirit and has no hands in the human sense. But if He has no hands, how can He intervene? And then the realization comes, we are His hands. Our prayer boomerangs back on us ... Lots of prayers are answered like that. So be warned![5]

Yet on a practical level, interpret it how one will, we cannot and should not delegitimize personal, petitionary prayer. Judaism, looking to the successful biblical examples of Hannah who prayed in bitterness of heart for a child and Moses who asked God in five short words for the recovery of his sister, asks us to put our needs and cares to God every day. The woman who prays for a sick relative, whether or not that is the only prayer she has said for a long time, certainly prays sincerely. It would be a heartless person indeed who failed to respect both her need and her fervent wish. It would be a brazen person who declared that prayer doesn't work like that. For God's ways are not our ways and God's will is, in the last analysis, a mystery beyond our understanding. Any prayer by any person of any religion in any language when uttered sincerely out of depth of feeling commands our total respect.

The problem is rather that in our times petitionary prayer is often the only form of prayer which many of us come to know about. For we base our understanding of prayer on what we are taught, which usually means what we learn as children, and on our experience of the community. If we are irregular attenders at services, or if at those services the worshippers are regularly distracted and there is an overall feeling of lack of concentration, then we have little opportunity of coming to realize that petitionary prayer has a sub-text more profound by far than the literal meaning of the words we say. And the text itself, the overt meaning of central portions of our liturgy, emphasizes human need on the one hand and God's power to satisfy it on the other. So what are we to think? Admittedly, God is to be praised when things go well, and much space in the prayer book is devoted to doing so, but at its most basic prayer regularly appears to be about asking from God. Thus the utilitarian ethic catches up even with prayer: Midas stretches out his hand towards it. Prayer, however, steadfastly refuses to turn into gold. It fails to comply; it simply will not be valued in that manner. But then, say some, if prayer will not oblige, give it up and reach out for something else.

But what, then, about God? If we don't get benefits in kind, does it mean that God doesn't listen to prayer, or are there other ways to find God in it, despite the apparent lack of results? Kushner, reinterpreting the purpose of prayer on the basis of what it can, rather than what it cannot, do, puts the matter in largely social and psychological terms. Prayer brings one the companionship and the comfort of the community with whom one prays. It strengthens the resolve to go on, it provides the deeper awareness that there are still things worth living for even after tragedy has struck.[6] Ultimately, though, what he describes are the consequences of the fact that prayer brings the closeness of the Presence of God. Kushner, a practising congregational Rabbi addressing the needs of the community, chooses to express this in terms of the inner benefits it brings to the suppliant. To the mystic, however, to the person concerned with the spiritual life for its own sake, the Presence of God is in itself more than enough: this is the ultimate goal and everything else feels trivial besides it. But both of them would agree that what prayer transforms is not the external, but the internal, reality of the person who prays. And when that happens, the outside world also appears different.

The Talmud understood this clearly when it considered the apparent contradiction between two traditions. Rabbi Hanin quoting Rabbi Hanina stated that whoever prayed at length would find that those prayers did not come back empty. But Rabbi Hiyya Bar Abba quoting Rabbi Yochanan said that, on the contrary, whoever prayed at length and thought about their prayers would get only heartache for their trouble.[7] As the Talmud notes, the crucial phrase on which the contradiction and its resolution depend is 'thought about'. On first reflection one might feel that the arguments should be just the other way round: surely the more one thinks about one's prayers, and the less one simply says them by rote, the better. But a closer analysis of what is meant by 'thinks about' brings one to the opposite conclusion. One should pray without 'thinking about' or, as the clause might be translated, 'speculating upon', the results of the activity; one cannot pester God as if God were a human being who must eventually yield to one's importunity.

The Tosafot, a group of commentators who love to note apparent difficulties and contradictions in the Talmud, make the point even more clearly. Surely, they observe, we have other instances in Rabbinic writing where 'thinking about' one's prayers is a good thing, so what can be wrong with it here? The answer they give is that here the phrase means 'to have a vested interest in the outcome of one's prayers', whereas in certain other contexts it simply means 'to direct one's heart to prayer'.[8] The message is clear: if one directs one's heart to prayer for its own sake one will indeed not return empty. But the fullness which one finds may be something other than the fulfilment of requests.

How then can we learn to pray, yet pray for something other? How can we pass beyond the 'failure of prayer', so that we come to know and share a deeper form of engagement with it which will not leave us empty or forsaken?

3. *The synagogue and the spirit*

Perhaps it is a sentimental illusion, but one senses that there was a time – and that there still are places where that time exists – when Jewish people knew where to go to talk to God and how to set about it. Zalman Shazar, third President of the State of Israel, recalls Yom Kippur in the Shtiebel, the small and intimate synagogue and community, where he grew up, when Reb Eliahu would lead the service:

> Entreaty began again in measured tones – and then low trilling, as if he were diving far down, sobbing as he struggled to rise, till at last he emerged triumphantly out of the depths and his voice was loud and clear as he trod the beaten path of the Reader's Repetition of the Amidah.
>
> How stirred one small boy was by this heartfelt praying!

Then we reached the sequence of 'the sins we have sinned', and the whole congregation moved, each within his Tallit, as the trees in a forest move when a storm passes over them.[9]

It is surely true that there was a time when the vast majority of the Jewish community was more at home in the synagogue, and felt closer to prayer, than it does today. The difference between then and now is that a distance has set in. This is partly a distance between us and the synagogue, and partly a distance between the synagogue itself and the art of prayer. The place where one talks to God has to feel like home. But the synagogue often doesn't. As a result, we often find it hard to bridge the gap between the language, style and expectations of our daily, secular lives and the concepts and vocabulary of the prayer book and the milieu in which we are expected to read it. Once, if the sacred tongue was not familiar, and it probably would have been, there was Yiddish. People could talk to God in a language like that, and they did! It bridged the gap between the sacred and the profane; home was neither the one nor the other, because everywhere the two worlds met. '*Guten Morgen zu Dir, Ribbono shel Olam* – Good morning to You, Master of the universe,' Rabbi Levi Yitzhak of Berditshev is said to have begun his famous Kaddish. English simply doesn't have the same resonance, not because words cannot be translated, but because the whole context of it, the way of life of the English speaking world, is different. It is our lives, even – or rather especially – our spiritual lives, which we find it difficult to translate.

The issue is not whether we are less sensitive people spiritually than we once were. Such generalizations are pointless: only God knows the secrets of the heart. Anyway my experience as a rabbi tells me that those who denounce the Jewish people of today for having little heart are not being fair. On the contrary, all people have existential concerns; many lead deep, but lonely, spiritual lives. The difficulty is one of context: it comes in trying to find the right way, and the right place, in which to share and develop this aspect of our existence. For we often express our spiritual lives through the media of Western society, by listening to great music, reading poetry, travelling amidst awe-inspiring scenery, discovering the state of our soul through the inward journey of psychoanalysis. Moved by all these things, none of which are particularly communal or specifically Jewish, we seek to develop that sense of inspiration further in the synagogue, only to find that the services simply don't help. How many times have I been told, or left to infer, the message that 'I can find God in nature', or 'I can find God in meditation', or 'I can find God in music', but I can't find God in the synagogue.

Inevitably, the synagogue responds to its changed position in Jewish life. Attended chiefly by people who feel culturally and socially more or less at home there, its centre of gravity may become cultural and social rather than spiritual. It is filled with people who may enjoy the service, but feel uncomfortable with prayer. In such an environment those who consciously seek a deepening of their spiritual life often find the atmosphere unconducive. As in the old joke in which the supposed worshipper notes that whereas Hymie may have come to synagogue to talk to God, he has come to synagogue to talk to Hymie, there are too many people who go to synagogue to talk chiefly to their neighbour rather than to God. This, together with the fact that most members of most synagogues lack a deep knowledge of the liturgy, in turn compels further changes. Thus, there is a risk that the service may become formalized and distanced from the worshippers; it is led for, rather than by, the congregation. Too few demands are made of worshippers; key prayers are said too quickly, key moments pass without the sense of collective concentration. It becomes easier to express oneself elsewhere.

Alternatively, the synagogue may recognize the difficulties and formulate a deliberate strategy of response. The language of prayer is changed; a major part of the service is said in the vernacular. There is an attempt to make the form of worship reflect the idiom of the day and draw from those sources of inspiration which act on a person in other areas of his or her life in our society. Fitting decorum is maintained. But inevitably there are losses. One senses that the argument of the opponents of early Reform was not disingenuous when they insisted, despite having authoritative sources of Jewish law against them, that it was wrong to say the central prayers in the vernacular. Nowadays, they argued, we have lost the art of translation. For there are, they maintained, levels of meaning concealed in every word of the prayers of our ancestors and these simply cannot be conveyed in any other language.[10] What they meant was that the liturgy comprises more than the words, than the melodies even, of which it is composed. Rather, it is a repository of the inner life and the aspirations not only of those who formulated it, but, just as significantly, of all those who ever prayed with it. The Hebrew words are thus imbued with the collective presence of the spiritual life of tens of generations, a vitality with which the individual worshipper, in uttering them, associates him or herself and by which he or she is strengthened and carried closer to God. For the fact is that one prays at least as much with the unconscious as with the conscious mind and the worshipper recognises intuitively an affinity with the well-worn page, even if on a rational level it may use language or express sentiments with which he or she does not agree.

One has to guard, however, against making generalized judgments which lead one to condemn any and every change in the service. There are many people who would argue that once a new liturgy, or the old liturgy in the vernacular, has become familiar, it too carries many levels of unconscious meaning and becomes imbued with the collective identity and spirituality of all those who have said it. They might add further that it is wrong, indeed totally unjustifiable, to repeat prayers the sentiments of which, racist or sexist perhaps, we would acknowledge to be offensive in any other context. Nevertheless, the following lines from a poem by Yaakov Cohen do, for all their sentimentality, describe the emotions of many a worshipper who seeks nothing more than to pray as his or her ancestors did:

> I pick up the ancient prayer book, withered by tears;
> To the Lord God of my fathers, their Refuge and their Rock of old, I call in my distress.
> In those same ancient words, seared by the pain of generations,
> I pour out my bitter speech, Let them, familiar with the paths on high, bear my complaint to
> God who dwells on high.

Radical changes may well be the mark of admirable courage, but the danger is that through them an important bond with the past may be loosened; one no longer immerses oneself when one prays in the same river as did our ancestors. The spiritual presence of the words may be less. A synagogue which prays largely in the vernacular may have taken a step towards its members, and it may have striven to narrow a gap, but in the end the gap cannot be narrowed from that side alone. It is a fact that a life of prayer makes certain demands and that it cannot be expected to 'work', however that may be defined, without a certain discipline. Many, furthermore, would consider that this includes an adherence to the traditional times, forms and language of our ancient tradition.

The danger, however, of discipline is that it all too easily becomes mere discipline, little more than the soulless performance of a routine. Prayer as habit has been much condemned. Already in the Mishnah Rabbi Eliezer says that a person who makes his prayer *keva* (the meaning of the term is open to debate, but probably means something like 'fixed' or 'set') does not offer real supplications.[11] The Talmud suggests various interpretations of this statement: what Rabbi Eliezer must have meant is that prayer shouldn't be a burden, or that it must be said with a true feeling of supplication, or that it shouldn't be done so much by rote that one cannot add any-

24

thing new to it. The probability is that Rabbi Eliezer was not opposed to habit, only to mere habit. For until something as important as prayer becomes habit, it is unlikely to become more than habit. This approach, adopted as normative practice by Jewish law, is not to be condemned as the condoning of hypocrisy, leading people to offer insincere prayers when they don't really feel like it. For just as a musician has to practise scales, not for their own sake, but so as to maintain such a level of technical familiarity as enables him or her to play and become immersed in great music, so too must we practise prayer. Jewish tradition requires us to do this, day in, day out. Certainly it has to be done on a serious and regular basis if we are to be able to express ourselves, or to lose ourselves, or to find God, in our prayers.

Unless we strive to make this possible, two problems will remain. Though we may be intellectually aware of the fact that prayer, cast as it largely is in the language of petition, is not so much about asking from God as about seeking for God, we will rarely gain access to any actual experience of that reality. And the world of the synagogue will not be one in which we feel sufficiently at home to recognize that here is the place where we come to talk to, to listen to, to deepen our experience of, God.

4. *The core and mature fruit of one's time* [12]

What is talking to God, and what are the fruits of such an endeavour? This is how Rabbi Shalom Noah Brosovsky expresses it in his elaboration of Maimonides' itemization of the different aspects of prayer. [13] Here he enlarges on what Maimonides means by saying that a person should 'utter supplication and pray every day', noting that this cannot refer to petitionary prayer because the master mentions this separately later.

> This, rather, is the very essence of the commandment [of prayer] – to pour out one's heart before the Holy, Blessed One, and to supplicate Him, – even when nothing at all

oppresses the heart. For we are not commanded to pray specifically when something oppresses us; rather the very act of supplication is to cleave to God and to pour out one's soul from a heart full of love into a loving heart. The meaning of this can be understood according to the explanation by our master, the author of Beit Avraham, may his memory protect us, of the verse 'and Esther continued and spoke further before the king ... and pleaded with him', which he understands to hint at the nature of prayer before the King of kings, the Holy, Blessed One, rendering it thus: '*sie hat sich gebeten zu ihm*',– that is, she pleaded with him, or rather for him, for she wanted him.[14]

Thus, the monologue of prayer becomes a dialogue of love; more boldly, the human being turns to God as the lover for whom wanting something from her partner is only a pretext for wanting him directly. Thus, pouring out our needs before God 'sweetens all the judgments'; it improves our portion because our beloved is with us in it, even if the bare facts which describe that portion have not changed. Hence Rabbi Shalom Noach continues:

> Even greater and more profound is the outpouring of the heart in prayer concerning spiritual matters, whether this be out of a feeling of longing and thirst for Him, blessed be He, or from oppression at the thought of how distant one has become from Him, blessed be His name, so that one cannot feel His nearness, or whether, heaven forbid, one has been caught up in evil desires until one feels confounded and ashamed to lift up one's face to Him and one pleads and pours out one's heart like water in prayer. There is no service of the heart greater than this.[15]

Furthermore, he adds, prayer of this kind is always answered, whereas there are reasons why prayers for material needs may not be.

The difference between the two types of prayer, for material as opposed to for spiritual needs, may be described as the difference between praying in order to get something out of one's relationship with God and praying in order to get into that relationship for the sake of nothing other than precisely that. One prays to be close to God because this is on one level the greatest privilege and the most wonderful experience the human being can know: as the Psalmist says, 'What else do I desire besides Thee on earth?' (73.25).

Of course, mood and motivation vary constantly. The Hasidic teachers were well aware of this when, alongside their emphasis on prayer for the sake of closeness to God, they stressed the fact that the state of a person's mind is in constant flux. Sometimes one's spiritual horizons are enlarged, sometimes they shrink to petty and selfish concerns, but they are never static. Thus when one's prayer life is going badly one can take hope from the fact that things will change. Certainly one must not give up.

In Rabbinic literature the key term used to describe concentration in prayer (and in all religious acts) is *kavvanah*. Translated as 'intention', or 'attention', *kavvanah* has been used in devotional literature to express an entire range of mental attitudes. At the most basic level Jewish law rules that prayer requires *kavvanah;* that is, the person engaged in prayer must know before Whom he or she is standing and what he or she is saying. Moving up the ladder of spiritual attainment, *kavvanah* comes to mean devotion and inwardness in prayer, hence spiritual concentration. Thus the Mishnah teaches that the pious of old used to meditate for an hour before praying, pray for an hour, and then meditate again for an hour afterwards in order to direct (*sheyechavvnu libbam*) their hearts to their Father in heaven.[16] To the Kabbalists, *kavvanah* becomes *kavvanot*, specific patterns of meditation upon particular aspects of the higher worlds engaged in by the initiated during prayer in order to create conduits for the flow of the Divine mercy. In Hasidic literature the term, simplified of such complexities, generally

27

means intense emotional and intellectual attachment to God in prayer; it is the necessary precondition for *devekut*, cleaving to the Divine.

One can take comfort, however, amidst all these high intentions, from a gloss to the *Shulchan Aruch* which indicates that although technically one is obliged to repeat one's prayers if one says them without *kavvanah*, in our day we do not do this because the likelihood is that the second time round we will do precisely the same again.[17]

Nevertheless, or perhaps precisely because it is so difficult, the issue of *kavvanah* is central for prayer. There is an infinite variety of states of mind. One should have a healthy respect for the person who said that he never got bored with prayer even though he did it three times each day because every time his attempts to concentrate fell short. Thus – and even the Talmud concedes this to be unavoidable[18] – one often prays without any concentration at all, realizing all of a sudden that one has finished the Amidah without having any memory of saying it at all. This has been likened to driving up outside one's house without having the faintest notion how one got home. But one shouldn't give up; at least the door is kept open, the access is kept clear. The habit is formed of keeping a period of time aside for the activity of prayer. Of course, there will be occasions when the 'duty' is resented, but how worthwhile it is in general to make time to stop and stare, to absent oneself from the rush of life, and seek silence instead of noise. At other times one thinks one's own thoughts, ponders or settles one's inner issues in the presence of God. Sometimes one is passionately concerned about a very real and tangible matter, and prayers for health, or for food, or for justice or for peace are said with a fervour quite different from yesterday when they were merely muttered by rote. Sometimes one prays close to a person, or to an experience, which so moves one that this feeling informs the whole of one's spirit. Sometimes one prays beneath the stars or among great mountains, or close to a tiny flower, and the remote concept that the world has a Creator becomes the immediate experience of wonder and awe. Sometimes one's words, borne on the wings of a scarcely conscious part of oneself, fly up in haste, leaving the spirit feeling purified and whole. Sometimes each word calls for particular attention, full of an inner life that only just before one had totally missed. Then the activity of saying the words of the prayers becomes, as Rabbi Nachman of Breslav describes it, like the gathering of flowers each one of which is a world in itself.[19] And sometimes one loses oneself; a greater sense of being has washed out the overwrought mind and cleansed the troubled heart.

5. 'Near is God to all who call to Him, to all who call to Him in truth' (Psalm 145.18)

What constitutes success in prayer? When can we say that it has worked? Perhaps it would be better to start with the opposite question: What, in this context, is failure? Failure, it seems to me, is when one leaves the synagogue, or ends one's prayers, with exactly the same things going round in the mind as when one started. None of one's preoccupations have shifted; the same mental baggage sits just as oppressively on the rack. But perhaps this is too hasty a judgment. Maybe such disappointments have to be seen in the light of a larger whole, for who can say what part such – for many of us all too frequent – occurrences play in the greater life of the spirit? Perhaps they, too, are part of the work. The only failure, then, is giving up, and even that may lead to a return to prayer at a later time or with a different spirit.

But what about success? It follows that it, too, must be described in terms of the whole, not just of a particular instance, of one's prayer life. Success is the desire to go on. It is the feeling that this spiritual relationship, however each of us may choose to describe it, of which prayer is a part, is worthwhile, that there is life in it, that to renege on the commitments it requires would constitute a great impoverishment. Success comes with the sense that there is life within the soul and with the intuition that there is vitality all about it and beyond. Success is the privilege of knowing that life has a further dimension than the material, or even than the emotional, world alone, and that in such a dimension what is distant becomes close; what is separate, one; what is mortal, part of what is vital, unending and recreated ever anew. How often does one glimpse such truths, how frequently does one intimate such things? Is it often, or only rarely – no more perhaps even than a handful of times in one's life? Of course the answer varies, from year to year, from person to person. But 'not very often' is frequently enough to change our priorities, to broaden our horizons and to alter totally our sense of what life means for the short period in which we are privileged to have it.

It may be asked, however, if such 'rewards' are sufficient for the person who turns to God in trouble and pours out his or her heart, only to find that disaster strikes precisely as predicted and that nothing is any different from how it would have been had God never been asked to help at all. Can one expect such a person to feel otherwise than disappointed? Harold Kushner addresses this issue in his book referred to above, and notes that whereas prayer will probably not stop the person one loves from 'dying right on schedule' (though the inexplicable sometimes does happen), that is not the same as saying that nothing is achieved. Prayer brings the solidarity of community and friends, resolve, the strength to start again.[20] But we cannot answer the question 'Why does God let this happen?'. Many and greater have tried.

Nevertheless, the following observations may be of some value. In tractate Berachot, the Talmud invokes and attempts to define the concept which has generally been known as 'the sufferings of love', though 'chastisements of love' would be a more accurate translation. These are trials which a person may undergo that cannot be explained (setting aside the question of how we might view such explanations) in terms of Divine punishment for any specific human deficiency or fault, but which express what has traditionally been understood as God's desire to test, and so improve, the human being. Given that in the particular instance there is indeed no cause for them in human sin, how are such evidently gratuitous sufferings to be defined? Are they always 'chastisements of love' or not? 'Rabbi Ya'akov bar Iddi and Rabbi Aha bar Hanina held different views. One said: Sufferings of love are sufferings which do not prevent one from studying the Torah ... The other said: Sufferings of love are sufferings which do not prevent one from being able to pray.' The Talmud concludes in the name of Rabbi Yochanan that they are both sufferings of love.[21] Technicalities aside, the distinction being made here is between sufferings which destroy the spirit and sufferings which do not. In all the positions here expressed the central idea is that the courage which enables a person to pray, or to study Torah, or, one might add, to engage in any other activity which affirms spiritual values despite adversity, transforms the process of endurance. It changes the dominance of bodily forces over the soul into a vindication of the powers of the spirit. Thus I recall a woman whose endeavour it was, despite the weakening of the muscles in her hand, to draw well a mother elephant with its baby. Not a particularly soulful task, one might have thought, yet through it she was able to show not only physical courage and self control, but a love for and an appreciation of life and all that is life giving, a generosity of spirit which never left her till she died.

Sometimes, of course, there is nothing a person can do; the very nature of the suffering involved is such that it robs him or her of all mental powers. Very often in such cases the greatest trials devolve upon the family, and it is they who are left seeking a way of comprehending their, and their dear one's, pain. It is then often they who show how, through courage and the persistence of the inner life, the human being can wrest meaning even from those elements of experience which cannot be justified according to any notion of fairness we can comprehend, and which are quite beyond our powers to explain.

Nobody, of course, can be expected to behave heroically all the time, though some people do: hours, minutes, of inner work are all of value. They vindicate the existence of a faculty which allows human beings to reach deeper than their own pain, to feel more broadly and compassionately than for themselves alone, to appreciate certain facets of life even amidst suffering, and to affirm that each of us is part of a greater whole than in our carelessness we often realize. I speak from the experience of others, which I have seen and by which I have been moved.

As for myself, like many people I do not find prayer easy, and I know that I often don't pray well. But one must keep trying. I believe in persistence. Just as it would be absurd to imagine that one could play beautiful music without regular and rigorous practice, so one can't expect to feel spiritually uplifted without constant, and often mundane, work. The traditional view of prayer as an activity for which frequent and regular times must be set aside deserves our respect, as should the requirement that our relationship with God be set within the framework of a morally and socially committed life. With regard to the results of prayer, we have to trust, on the basis of the experience of others, and occasionally in limited measure from our own, that the inner life, the Divine vitality, the river, is real.

Thus we recognize perhaps the description by Rav Kook of prayer as the articulation of that life force which flows through all being and unites it with its source in God. It is not alien to us; instinctively the heart assents to his words. But we know that for the most part this is not our everyday experience: such knowledge is a privilege and a special reward. Most of us, for most of the time, are conscious of living in a world where at best, in Heschel's words, God is not at home. The absence, of course, is in our perception, but for all that it is no less real. From the Midrashic through to the Hasidic tradition evil and cruelty are described as forces which push away the Presence of God; the

Prayer

Shechinah can no longer abide in the world. The task of prayer is to draw it back again, to change our hearts and thereby our values and our deeds, so that we work with greater commitment for a world in which 'they shall not hurt nor destroy in all My holy mountain, for the earth shall be full of the knowledge of the Lord, as the waters cover the sea' (Isaiah 11.9).

In the meantime I believe with Leah Goldberg that:

Even to those as small as me,
One among tens of thousands,
Even to the children of affliction
On the shores of disappointment ...
The river calls in love.

II

Torah

... And all day long amongst the letters of the Gemara,
In the ray of light, in the shape of the bright cloud,
In the purest of my prayers and the clearest of my thoughts,
In my sweetest meditations and in my greatest pain –
My soul has only sought that You should show yourself,
Just You, You, You ...

(Chaim Nachman Bialik)

1. Doubts and questions

It is an old rabbinic truism that there are seventy faces to the
Torah. For the Torah speaks about many subjects and people's
responses to them are rich and varied.

In the first place, the word Torah itself may mean many
things. It may be used in a general sense to refer to the whole
of Jewish life, learning, lore and practice, folk history and
nostalgia included, thus constituting in both a sentimental and
more serious sense everything that forms our 'roots'. More particularly, Torah may be used to mean the corpus of law, written
and oral, which defines how the Jew is to behave in all con-
ceivable – and many inconceivable – situations, thus constituting a body which speaks with the voice of authority and seeks
to define our life in all its details. More specifically still, Torah,
or the Torah, is used to refer to the Chummash, the five books
traditionally understood to have been dictated directly by God
to Moses on Mount Sinai and during the journeying of the
people of Israel in the desert. Finally, to most people the Torah
is the Scroll kept in the Ark in the Synagogue and from which

we read on Shabbat and Festivals. Each of these uses of the word elicits a different response. It is difficult therefore to talk about Torah as if it were one specific, single subject, and the movement backwards and forwards between different meanings, natural and inevitable even in a casual conversation on the subject, will of course be reflected in the discussion below.

Yet the various ways in which the word Torah is used are not nearly as diverse as people's reactions to it. For some, Torah is the unquestionable manifestation of the Divine will which rules our lives. The challenge it presents is one of knowledge and obedience; the problems are ignorance and weakness of will, not religious or moral doubt, let alone intellectual dissent. To others, Torah is what one has learned to compromise with: 'this I keep and this I don't'. Such an attitude may be based on the pragmatic admission that 'others are more religious than I am', or it may be accompanied by a more or less latent sense of guilt. It may be founded on an ignorance about which we feel a complacent lack of concern, or on the painful consciousness that want of knowledge deprives us of the ability to develop and deepen our Jewish life. The study of Torah may be something which we aspire to do more of, something which we don't care about one way or the other, or something from which we are held back by general unease or even specific, conscious doubts.

With regard to the latter, there are many areas of difficulty. How can I relate to the different concepts, the apparently distant and different reality, of which the Torah speaks? How am I expected to make sense of the way in which in the Torah God simply stretches out an arm and intervenes in history when there is little sign of God's doing that today? How can one escape the conclusion that either the world, or God, or both are different now, and what impact does that have on the degree to which we find the Torah relevant to our own lives? Furthermore, the Torah is traditionally understood to be the expression of the eternal will of God, yet some of its commandments seem alien and even ugly to us today. The Torah is indeed inspiring in many of its prescriptions, but are we traitors if we admit that in other areas it leaves us troubled and uneasy? To what extent are we free today to interpret its laws and redefine the areas of their application? The rabbis of old, for example, found the means to extend or extenuate the circumstances in which many biblical injunctions were to be carried out. But if we have such powers, how do we find an appropriate balance between obedience to the dictates of our tradition and the right, if there is such a thing, to reconsider? What then should we make of the absolute claim for its own authority which we find stated repeatedly in the Torah? Can we, finally, believe that meaning is to be discovered in those lengthy sections of the Torah which deal with rituals that have ceased to be kept for almost two thousand years, such as the details of the Temple observances, and of the sacrifices in particular? How are we to find significance in material apparently so recondite, irrelevant and unappealing? Some of these issues may be fodder for the atheist and others grist to the anti-Semite's mill, but they remain for all that food for the serious and committed follower to chew on. The questions they raise inform the discussion that follows. I trust that as we wrestle with them, we will also uncover for ourselves the Torah which is and always has been the source of moral and spiritual challenge, and that the more we learn, the more we will feel engaged.

As if these considerations were not enough to grapple with, we also have to take into account the fact that relatively few of us are clear and consistent in our attitudes, especially when it comes to so complicated a subject as religion. Our responses to Torah are, therefore, neither unequivocal nor unchanging. Most of us experience conflict, at least at some level. Most of us harbour more than a degree of ambivalence, having a love of Torah and a yearning to come closer to our people and our God on the one hand, and doubts, criticisms and the impulse to reject or withdraw on the other. What one part of us loves another part may at the same time fear; equally, what the mind may not believe in, heart or history or both may well lead us to practise. Furthermore, these feelings are not governed by ourselves alone: the welcome or rejection we experience in our own community, the openness or hostility of surrounding society, our self-consciousness or ease as Jews, may well determine attitudes which we then regard as conscious and deliberate decisions. It is a mistake to think of our identity as a single and static thing. For most of us the answer to the question 'Who am I?' is subject to change, and our understanding of who we are is as much the product of unsettled conflicts as of facts and resolutions. All this will influence our attitudes to Torah.

I do not exempt myself from any of the dilemmas and complications outlined above. When I was a child at Cheder, religion school, I enjoyed many of my lessons but, like so many others, I from time to time rebelled against the study of a subject which in my ignorance I sometimes considered a burden and a bore. (This was, of course, the fashionable thing to do.) Though I always loved the way we celebrated Shabbat and the festivals at home, I had little notion of the joy that was to be found in Jewish learning. True, I used to hear my grandfather, a rabbi by vocation and by love who gave his first sermon when he was three to his little brother and his last when he was in his late eighties to a large congregation in Berlin, quote the verse of the Psalmist, 'Songs have your statutes become to me in the house of my estrangement' (119.54). But I could make no connection with the words. I had limited experience of the music of Torah and, fortunately, none of estrangement. Now, however, I feel differently. Little by little I have discovered what solace the study of Torah can bring in a life full of rushing around and restless activity. I have begun to find in it both music and restoration and, hidden among its letters, the quiet company of those teachers and fellow students who have walked its paths before me. I understand my grandfather better and appreciate the living memory and inspiration he has left me. It has helped me to perceive in the features of Torah I once found complex and distant a vital, penetrating wisdom which challenges and moves me. It is this discovery which motivates me as I write this chapter.

2. *The need for trust*

No Rabbi can accept the idea that the study of the Torah is simply another academic discipline. Torah addresses itself to the heart as much as to the mind, to what we do as much as to how we think and what we feel. It is all-embracing; it defines a way of life and seeks to direct its practitioners along that path. As such it asks first and foremost for our trust; the assent of our intellect is important, indeed some would say essential, but is not of itself sufficient. For the Torah requires that we follow its precepts, that we study it not only to know and to understand it, but also and especially so as to practise it and live by it. There is a profound difference between the two goals of studying in order to know and studying in order to practise. So long as we are engaged in the former only, the mind is in control of its object; but as soon as we are required to live according to the results of what we learn, the mind is obliged to yield its command and make way for experiences the nature of which it cannot predetermine or predict. Instead of being the questioner, remote and aloof, we find ourselves questioned and called upon to respond. Heart and conscience are increasingly engaged; our desire to know about religion and God is humbled by the increasing awareness that the more relevant fact is that God knows us. Judaism asks us to enter into this dialogue, though we may well choose to begin it gradually and with caution. Afterwards it develops a momentum of its own, but beginning such a process requires a great deal of trust.

Why, though, should we have to show such trust? Why should we, who set so much store by the right to make our own decisions, cede our autonomy and follow a path which we cannot possibly understand at the outset? There are, of course, many for whom this is not an issue. Brought up in observant homes, they have lived according to halachah, the discipline of Jewish law, all their lives. Questioning, if it comes at all, comes later. Thus they would see the 'problem' as the perspective of an outsider and might be inclined to say to one who experiences such difficulties: 'It is the will of God. Just follow and you will understand later.' But there are others, both among those born, and amidst those who have come later, to traditional Judaism, who would recognize the need to respond to this modern dilemma.

One answer might be to consider what it is that Judaism asks of us. For it doesn't require us only to think about life in a particular way. It educates us to respond to the whole world with the whole person. In order that we should be equipped to do this, it endeavours to foster in us certain sensibilities, notably greater awareness of the moral, and deeper consciousness of the spiritual aspects of life. This cannot be achieved simply by telling us that these dimensions exist; we have to be put in touch with the actual experience of such matters. What Judaism wants to teach us is therefore something which we have to be led to discover, an understanding of which we must arrive at, for ourselves. Hence the challenge Judaism faces is not merely that of informing its adherents of the truths in which it believes but, far more significantly, that of guiding them to perceive those matters for themselves. This, from one point of view, is the purpose of what in Judaism has always been *the* path *par excellence*, the way of the commandments. Through the commandments, the mitzvot, the framework is created by which we make ourselves available to certain experiences that have the power to educate our spirits and refine the manner in which we live our lives. 'To say that the Mitzvot have meaning is less accurate than saying that they lead us to wells of emergent meaning, to experiences which are full of hidden brilliance of the holy, suddenly blazing in our thoughts', writes A. J. Heschel.[1] For example, we set aside the Shabbat, make it holy, protect it from invasion by the quotidian concerns of money, manufacture and chores. We enter its special world, within time but outside ordinary time, 'partaking of the nature of the world to come', as our Rabbis put it, not to act but to be acted upon. For the end to which we observe its special laws is certainly not so that we can show off our own scrupulousness. It is rather to follow in a sacred tradition which has taught, with an insight refined over the course of millennia, how a day can best be protected and made special, so as to make ourselves accessible to the opportunities for spiritual growth which such sanctified time can offer. As for what we will actually learn or gain from the experience, that is, in the very nature of things, a matter we cannot know in advance.

A story is told about two students who meet at the crossroads between Vilna and Mezeritch some time in the 1760s. Vilna was at that period famed as the home of the Gaon Elijah, whose austere way of life, brilliance of mind and phenomenal Talmudic learning had caused his fame to spread throughout the lands of the dispersion. With the death of the Ba'al Shem Tov, Mezeritch, home of its second leader Dov Baer, had become the centre of the rapidly expanding Hasidic movement. 'Where are you going?', asked the one student of the other. 'I'm going to Vilna to sit at the feet of the Gaon and learn to master the Torah,' came the reply. 'And what about you?', he inquired in turn. 'I'm going to Mezeritch to Dov Baer to learn to let the Torah master me,' responded the first.

To some degree at least we all must learn to allow the Torah to master us. Though it is obviously important to examine the beliefs and practices of Judaism carefully, even critically, there comes a point where we have to go further. This does not mean that we must act unthinkingly, dismiss all doubt or surrender our mind, but it does mean that we have eventually to commit ourselves and act. Otherwise we remain onlookers, and religion is something which has to be lived. Judaism, like gardening in the familiar joke, cannot remain a thing most people prefer to turn over in their minds. If we wish to follow a spiritual path we may not remain aloof. There is a time, however carefully we prepare ourselves for it, when an act of letting go is inevitable. The journey may be contemplated by anyone, but its joys and hardships are understood only by the person who travels on the way. For the experience will be other than the preconception, and the issues it raises not necessarily those that were foreseen. This is the force of the principle which has become axiomatic in Judaism: *'na'aseh venishma* – we will do and then we will hear' (Exod. 24.7). In other words, we recognize that we must first acquire experience and we trust that understanding will follow later.

The full significance of these words, *na'aseh venishma*, can only be appreciated if we take them in their original context. They are the collective response of the whole people at Mount Sinai. At the supreme moment of revelation they form a declaration of faith. This may at first sight seem strange; after all, they contain no dogma, demand no adherence to particular ideals, constitute no platform. What they are is a statement of trust. They affirm the willingness to follow, to embark on a journey together even though at the start there can be limited knowledge only of the end of that journey, for the meaning of the voyage is contained in the travelling itself. The readiness to trust which these words express may rarely if ever have been stated so publicly since, but their importance is confirmed whenever each of us determines to deepen our engagement with our spiritual tradition. They mark our preparedness to assay, to 'taste and see' (Psalm 34.9). The inner readiness they articulate is similar whether it comes in the context of a decision finally reached after months of hesitation to begin to light candles on Friday night, or in that of the determination to engage more frequently in prayer or to observe the festivals or fast days more strictly. The heart says 'I will be open, I will listen to this experience'. Thus the person who takes the first steps on the journey and the person who takes the hundredth step have much in common; so do the one who never dares and the one who always knows it all beforehand. The former pair may discover new spaces, the latter never can. What will fill those spaces, what the fruits of our daring will be, no one can possibly know in advance. Indeed, it is precisely this preparedness not to know, this readiness to enter into an experience to which we will be subject, that defines the essential steps. It is, as it were, in our moments of openness, in our undefended spaces, that God can find and speak to us. We therefore seek to learn more, not solely for the purpose of gaining greater knowledge but also in order to experience once again the state of not knowing; we seek to practise more, to pray more, in order to stand at the threshold and greet that which is not in or of ourselves alone. Faith may be defined in this context as the trust that the experience, the relationship into which we allow ourselves to enter, is of value. Doubt and hesitation are not the opposite of faith but rather its inevitable, necessary partners. Its real contraries are arrogance and a closed heart, the conviction that we know it all. Indeed, the blind, unquestioning conviction that we have got it right can be a greater barrier to trust in God than the honest uncertainties of the genuine seeker.

How, then, can we find the readiness to 'let Torah master us'? The answer must lie in developing the confidence to trust that it is not a void that we enter but a tried and tested path we follow. 'It is a tree of life to those that grasp it; those who hold to it are happy. Its paths are paths of pleasantness and all its ways are peace.' Thus runs the prayer we say whenever we return the Torah Scroll to the Ark. But how are we to know? For me, and I conclude this section on an avowedly personal note, the answer lies partly in the intuitions of the human heart and partly in the example others have set. It is surely not fortuitous that the prayer from which I have just quoted should refer to the Torah through the image of the tree. Who can be immune in the presence of nature, the cold dew on a spider's web or the winter sun in the branches of a witch hazel, to the sense of wonder or to the feeling of spiritual affinity with something infinitely greater than the self? In human company also, in unanticipated moments of understanding, the perception overtakes us that we live our separate lives in the context of a greater life that both unites and transcends our own. Faith, for a moment, becomes firm knowledge. Part of the relationship between such intuitions and the way of Torah is that the latter, by purifying our lives morally and disciplining and fostering them spiritually, has the power to make us increasingly more sensitive to such instants, turning occasional intuitions into an attitude which guides and governs all we do.

There are those who seek absolute proof. No perfect formula can be furnished. What we have, however, is something of far greater value: testimony, living evidence accumulated over thousands of years that the path of Torah can lead us to a greater awareness of God. It comes from people, from the quality of the lives led by those who genuinely strive to abide by their faith. Amidst the moments in other lives I have as a communal rabbi been privileged to share, I have been particularly moved by contacts with a number of remarkable older people, none of them at all ostentatious, whose faith has sustained them through many and varied tribulations. I know, for example, a man who walks very slowly with two sticks but would never miss a Shabbat in synagogue. I met him once on his way to the park:

'Can I help you over the road?'
'No, thank you. The Almighty has blessed me and I still have one tenth of my sight.'
'Do you need anything in your home?'
'No, thank you. The Almighty has blessed me with a good wife and family.'
'Is there anything at all we can do for you?'
'No, thank you. The Almighty has blessed me with a long life and with everything I need.'

On the other hand, I find little compelling in the citation of a hundred verses as proof that the Torah has to be true and that

God must surely exist. The attempt to do so from word games with Scripture and on computer screens is a trivialization unworthy of the issue. Likewise I am suspicious of those who claim to know for certain that there is a God and who turn that knowledge into a battery of dogmatic assertions. Miracles leave me uneasy and at accounts of wonders my thoughts often turn to those for whom there was no rescue and whom God's mercies never seemed to reach. I find little power of motivation in promises and imprecations, although I believe deeply that the life lived according to Torah is rewarding. But faith and panaceas are entirely different things. Theoretical religion, ignorant of the realities of the heart, is a dangerous thing. The world is full of religious bigots whose stubborn adherence to the rules of their systems has given them a pernicious belief in the infallibility of their own position. There are plenty of pietists who exploit tradition, who manipulate the trust of the uncritical and preach love while rousing hate. But none of this can erase the evidence of what good people have done and of the courage with which many have confronted the harsh demands of life through the strength they have drawn from their faith.

Judaism is in this sense a religion of example; it asks us to follow in the footsteps of those who have travelled before us and grown wise along the way. This is expressed in the opening lines of our most basic prayer, which appeals not to the God of absolute truth of whose existence we are required to be sure and certain, but rather to the God of Abraham and Sarah; of Isaac and Rebecca; Jacob, Rachel and Leah; to the God of all who have followed in their path since. The value of Torah is vindicated neither in abstruse knowledge nor in dialectics, but in experience, in life itself.

3. *Study of Torah as a pathway to God*

It is not only the performance of the commandments, but also the study of the Torah, which brings us into the presence of

God. In the previous section the focus was largely on practice; here the emphasis will be on learning. Judaism, after all, ascribes unequalled importance to Talmud Torah, to Jewish study. Our rabbis teach us that there are many commandments the reward for which has no limits, such, for example, as giving to the needy, respecting the dead, visiting the sick and making peace between people who have fallen out. But it is Talmud Torah, the study of Torah, which leads to the practice of them all.[2] Clearly, then, the significance of learning is that it both enables the student to know what is right and imbues him or her with the desire to do it. But Talmud Torah has a deeper purpose as well.

It might be considered that this deeper purpose is knowledge and the love of learning itself. After all, Judaism values knowing: great respect is accorded to the scholar, the community turns to those who know the details of the tradition, authority and decision-making powers are conferred upon the learned. Indeed, Judaism knows of no higher goal than to spend one's time in the study of the words of the Torah, 'for they are our life and the length of our days, and we will meditate on them day and night' (the evening service). We venerate the memory of the great sages who lived their lives in literal accord with this ideal. We recognize also that it is not just to the brilliant scholars and teachers but to the broad mass of Jews throughout the ages who devoted themselves to learning out of the sheer love of learning that we owe the form and fabric of traditional Jewish life. Indeed it is one of the beauties of Judaism that Jewish society is not at heart premised upon material achievements and the consequent hierarchies of wealth and rank, but upon knowledge of and dedication to Torah.

It is, therefore, an undeniably noble goal to seek to learn for the sake of knowing. Nevertheless, knowledge itself is not necessarily the ultimate motivating factor for the student of Torah, because knowledge alone is not the ultimate object of Torah study. For how, if that were the case, could the Talmud object as it does (and the comment is applied to study as well as to practice) 'Have we not said: it is all the same whether one does much or whether one does little, so long as the heart is directed towards Heaven.'[3] There is, therefore, clearly something more than quantity at issue; the aim of Torah study has to be something greater than the amassing of knowledge.

Perhaps, then, we have to consider that the end of learning is not only action, but also learning itself; that it is the endeavour itself and not only the fruit of the endeavour, which is of value. There is a deep truth in this idea. To the genuine student of Torah it usually matters little what the topic is with which he or she is engaged and whether or not it is relevant to the practicalities of life as a Jew. The activity may have no immediate purpose other than the joy of doing it. After all, are not our sacred texts the record of our encounter with God as understood by our greatest teachers in each generation, and is not the opportunity to study them an unequalled privilege, being perhaps that occupation in which we come as close as a human being can to the discovery of God's will. Learning is not therefore the means alone, the way of acquiring the knowledge necessary for engaging in religious activity; in itself it already is such activity. This may seem an absurd claim when confronted with many of the classic volumes of Jewish literature, the Talmud, Maimonides and the Shulchan Aruch, with their commentaries and super-commentaries which daunt all but the initiated. I certainly would have thought so, did think so for a long time. But after a while one comes to sense, in passages which deal with issues which one might have imagined could never ever interest one, the subject-matter of which was already academic even when it was first discussed some two thousand years ago, that there is here a different kind of attraction than the overt appeal – or lack of it – of the topic itself, a deeper current of thought and feeling than that which provides the obvious and immediate form of the piece in question. One feels the presence of a spiritual pressure, a quest for the knowledge of God along even the most minute paths as they are penetrated by the exploration of what might be the Divine will in this or that or the other eventuality, regardless of the likelihood of those particular circumstances coming into being. Indeed, one begins to appreciate that it is possible to wear out the mind upon apparently abstruse paths of enquiry precisely in order to discover that which lies beyond the mind, not in order to know but so as to enter into the presence of the One who knows.

Thus, in parallel with the approach to study which stresses the discovery of the will of God, we find a further attitude which puts the focus more overtly on the sense of God within the material studied. This is articulated most clearly in Hasidic thought. Hence, for example, in the ethical will of the Ba'al Shem Tov, the founder of the movement, the student of Torah is given the following advice: 'When one speaks during the period of study, one should have no other thought in mind than [the desire to] cleave to the Creator, blessed be He.' The author adds that concentration on the subject of study will lead to a due sense of connection with God.[4] Hence the key term *devekut,* by which is described in Hasidic thought the whole longing of the soul to be close to and cleave to God, is applied to the purpose of study. This approach could perhaps have been inferred from the Talmudic dictum quoted earlier that 'it is all the same whether one does much or whether one does little, so long as the heart is directed towards Heaven'. But in Hasidic thought it is spelled out. The end is not the learning, but the orientation of the heart, not the substance of what is studied but the relationship with God which engagement with Torah may foster. The purpose of study, like that of prayer, is to serve as a meeting place where spirit and the life of all spirit may encounter one another. However important any other aspects of learning may be, they remain secondary. One learns Torah to be brought into contact with the presence of God.

Clearly, though, both of the latter approaches to study presuppose a certain attitude of mind. Taking the phrase from the

Torah, the Talmud calls this *Yirat Shamayim,* the fear of Heaven. (The way in which the term is used makes it clear that the negative connotations of the English word 'fear', suggesting as it does the dread of punishment, are not intended. 'Awe in the face of Heaven' would therefore be a better translation; but 'fear of Heaven' is an established and accepted phrase and not, therefore, easily replaced.) In a famous passage[5] three comparisons are made to illustrate the importance of this quality by showing how worthless the achievements are of those who study much but have no sense of awe. In the first, an analogy is made 'to the case of a man who says to his steward "store this *kor* (a large quantity) of wheat in the attic". The steward went and did so. The man said to him "Did you mix in a *kav* (a small amount) of preserving salts?" The steward replied that he hadn't. "It would have been better," said the man, "if you hadn't stored the wheat for me."' Torah without the fear of Heaven, the analogy implies, may well be worse than useless; unless it is assimilated with an appropriate attitude and deployed in the right way, religious knowledge becomes noxious and rots. The Talmud continues: 'Rabbah, son of Rav Huna, said: "A person who knows Torah but has no fear of Heaven is like a treasurer who has been given the keys to the inner chamber while those to the outer chamber have been withheld from him. How is he to get in?" Rabbi Yannai declared: "Alas for the person who builds a gate to land he has not got."' At first sight it may appear that Rabbah and Rabbi Yannai are saying the same thing, but there is in fact a subtle difference between them. According to the former, Torah is indeed the inner chamber. In Torah resides the secret of religious experience; only it cannot be reached except by the person who approaches it in the right spirit. But his colleague goes further. Torah itself is no more than a gateway; what really matters is what it opens on to – the threshold of the fear of Heaven.

What, however, is the fear of Heaven? Maimonides asks the same question in *The Laws of the Foundations of the Torah*:

'What is the way that will lead to the love of God and to the fear of God?' He answers:

> When a person contemplates His great and wondrous works and creatures and from them obtains a glimpse of His wisdom which is incomparable and infinite, he will straightway love Him, praise Him, glorify Him, and long with an exceeding great longing to know His great Name; even as David said, 'My soul thirsts for God, for the living God' (Psalm 42.3). And when he ponders these matters, he will recoil frightened, and realize that he is a small creature, lowly and obscure, endowed with slight and slender intelligence, standing in the presence of Him who is perfect in knowledge.[6]

Fear of Heaven is thus defined as the step backwards which follows the step forwards; it is the sense of awe which overcomes the soul when it apprehends the greatness of God and the wondrous nature of the works that fill the world. It is the response of the open heart to its place within the majesty of creation, the realization of the spirit that it stands before a presence infinitely greater than itself, of which it has nevertheless the privilege of being aware.

In what could almost be regarded as a modern sequel to Maimonides' description, Anatole Shcharansky wrote about his experience of studying the Book of Psalms during his lonely confinement in Chistopol prison:

> In the course of time, one begins to understand that fear of God is a result of an inner stirring brought about by the lofty Divine vision, by a feeling of submission and respect for God's essence, and especially by the instinctive, subconscious fear of man to expose himself as being unsuited for this lofty role and as being unworthy of being chosen for this task with his meagre talents.[7]

If these are the feelings which it can engender, the study of the Torah is clearly no mere academic exercise. The emphasis may be placed on the diligence of the mind or on the receptivity of the heart or alternately on both, but in no case is the ideal purpose knowledge alone, so much as knowledge of God. One studies Torah to come as near as the human being can to the discovery of God's will, to the realization of God's presence.

4. *Authority and autonomy*

In the two preceding sections stress has been laid on the need for humility so as to be prepared to 'taste and see' (Psalm 34.9). This approach is based on the tacit assumption that in matters of religion we have the right to choose the degree of our commitment and the level of our observance for ourselves. But is such a premise justified? Does Judaism accord us the right to choose? It may be argued that in today's society the question is theoretical only, because all Jews do in effect choose the way in which they practise their religion, if only by virtue of the fact that there are other options available to them which they do not pursue. But at the level of principle there are issues here which cannot be ignored. The question of choice presents us with a paradox: how can we choose that which claims to command? In considering this question we are inevitably led to a second: what importance do we ascribe to reason and the decision making faculties in helping us to determine what we should do?

Our historical situation makes these issues particularly difficult for us. We have to face dilemmas which for earlier generations were certainly less prominent and for some may not have existed at all. Traditional Judaism does not reveal to us a variety of possible paths of which we freely select the one or the other; it presents us with a sophisticated system of commandments, by which every moment of our life is governed. Admittedly, there are many ways of understanding the commandments and a wealth of traditions regarding the details of how we put them into practice, but there is no free choice with regard to the central principle of their acceptance. There exist only obedience and disobedience. But in today's society this is a difficult proposition to accept. The freedom to choose, to arrive at our own decisions, to follow our own judgment uncoerced, is justifiably important to us. It lies at the foundation of the ideal of the democratic society, which emphasizes the autonomy of the individual and the right to pursue our own goals within the limits prescribed by the need to provide the same freedoms for others. By contrast, the readiness to do what one doesn't understand, to subject oneself to the will of God, to be bound by sacred law in letter and in spirit, is an essential feature of the traditional religious community. Unless we are prepared to sacrifice entirely either the one or the other, we will almost inevitably experience repeated tensions as these two conceptions of society and systems of value pull us in opposing directions.

It is with the Enlightenment, and in particular in the approaches of the rabbis and leaders who had to contend with the changes in Jewish society occasioned by it, that this conflict comes fully to the fore in Jewish thought. Samson Raphael Hirsch must be reckoned among the great defenders of traditional Judaism. He asserted the authority of Judaism in the face of the new 'enlightened', universalist values and strove to maintain the cohesiveness of orthodox practice in a period, the mid-nineteenth century, when new opportunities in the non-Jewish world were exerting an increasingly erosive influence on Jewish observance. Whilst affirming the universalist ideal and the place of the Jew in society as a whole, he staunchly defended the stance of orthodoxy in an article entitled with deliberate irony 'Judaism Up To Date':

Let us not deceive ourselves. The whole question is simply this. Is the statement 'And God spoke to Moses saying', with which all the laws of the Jewish Bible commence, true or not true? Do we not really and truly believe that God, the Omnipotent and Holy, spoke thus to Moses? Do we speak the truth when in front of our brethren we lay our hand on the scroll containing these words and say that God has given us this Torah, that His Torah, the Torah of truth and with it of eternal life, is planted in our midst? If this is to be no mere lip-service, no mere rhetorical flourish, then we must keep and carry out this Torah without omission and without carping, in all circumstances and at all times. This word of God must be our eternal rule superior to all human judgment, the rule to which all our actions must at all times conform; and instead of complaining that it is no longer suitable to the times, our only complaint must be that the times are no longer suitable to it.[8]

There is no mistaking the polemical bent of Hirsch's words. They were first published in 1854, less than a decade after the relatively new movement of Reform had held its conference in Hirsch's very own city of Frankfurt. On this occasion Rabbi David Einhorn, admittedly one of the more radical spokesmen, had stated in a discussion on Messianism, an issue then critical to Jewish self-definition, that: 'Now our concepts have changed. There is no need any more for an extended ceremonial law ... Only the Talmud moves in circles; we, however, favour progress.'[9]

In the late twentieth century the debate has not gone away. Indeed these present decades may be described as a period of harsh reappraisal of the impact of the Enlightenment upon traditional Judaism. Thus Yeshayahu Leibowitz pugnaciously asserts a position somewhat similar in this respect to that of Hirsch. The Jew, he argues, must obey the commandments; the Jew must do so for no other cause than that such is the will of God:

Every reason given for the Mitzvot that bases itself on human needs – be they intellectual, ethical, social, or national – voids the mitzvot of all religious meaning. For if the Mitzvot are the expression of philosophic knowledge, or if they have any ethical content, or if they are meant to benefit society, or if they are meant to maintain the Jewish people, then he who performs them serves not God but himself, his society or his people. He does not serve God but uses the Torah of God for human benefit and as a means to satisfy human needs.[10]

In short, any attitude towards the commandments which is based on anything other than complete acceptance and obedience, however noble the vision by which it is inspired, be it spiritual perfection or the betterment of society, and however many of the precepts of the Torah it may lead one to perform, is ultimately a betrayal of the readiness to follow the will of God.

What are we to make of these arguments? Clearly, there are many problems with the kind of extreme stance taken by thinkers such as Hirsch and Leibowitz. In the first place it may be objected to on purely historical grounds. Is it actually true to the facts of how Judaism has developed? Might it not be argued that our understanding of what is meant by performing the will of God has indeed been mediated by human judgment, and still is? Even if one were to take the view that every letter of the written Torah was literally dictated by God, this Torah has been subject to constant interpretation, and, one might add, will surely have to be so in the future if it is to answer the new questions which will inevitably arise with the passage of time. Thus the human role in the development of Jewish law cannot be so readily dismissed. Once, furthermore, it is conceded that the development of halachah reflects human concerns, the values that underlie them, such, for example, as the good of society and the pursuit of justice, cannot be regarded as irrelevant. On the contrary, one cannot but ask what the reasons behind and the purposes served by Jewish practices are, and then Leibowitz' absolute position ceases to make sense.

In the second place one has to ask whether it is either wise, or even in accord with the traditional Jewish view of human nature, to invite the suspension of judgment. According to

Jewish tradition it is precisely by means of the faculty of reason and the capacity for making choices based on its use that God differentiated us from the rest of creation. How then can one simply take this most precious of gifts and determine not to use it? Would not such submission constitute a surrender of precisely that freedom which God wants us to employ in the service of the Divine, a sort of mental equivalent of the return to Egypt, a land in which we could not receive the Torah because the Torah is not given to slaves? Against this it has been argued that we make God small, as it were, that we reduce the Divine to our size by insisting on looking at God through the lens of our limited mental capacities. But it is hard to see how one could do otherwise. The interposition of our reasoning process may at times indeed create a barrier between ourselves and Heaven, but it is an essential part of our attempt to comprehend what Heaven requires of us and to understand the meaning and purpose of our lives. When, furthermore, we are taught that '*Rachamana liba ba'ei* – the Merciful One desires the heart', we may legitimately claim that this means precisely what it says: that God wants us, with and despite our sensitivities and our difficulties and our faults. The Rebbe of Kotsk was presumably not limiting its application to human relationships when he coined the saying: 'If I am I because I am I, and you are you because you are you, then I am I and you are you. But if I am I because you are you, and you are you because I am I, then I am not I and you are not you.'[11] If a person has no space to be him- or herself, then not only does that person suffer, but, it might also be said, there is a deeper, spiritual loss. For the portion of the Divine life he or she might have perceived, that aspect of the creativity of the Creator which he or she might have brought to expression, is lost.

Texts aside, plain experience also tells us that it is highly dangerous to invite the suspension of the critical faculties. Were it to be argued that this is intended to apply to 'the word of God' only, one would have to answer that it is hard to invite the suspension of judgment in certain cases: once dismissed the power of discrimination is not easily recalled. Furthermore, 'the word of God' is a phrase notoriously open to abuse, especially if one considers that in most religious groups this 'word' generally reaches the populace through the mediation of a clergy among which, as well as the genuine and the great, there may be those who are intolerant, unintelligent, bigoted or downright unscrupulous. The long and bloody history of religious wars proves the point.

But many thinkers would take the argument against Hirsch and Leibowitz further still. For to many the idea that the Torah is literally the word of God, a kind of divine dictation, is no longer seen as tenable. Hence the human element in the very earliest and the most holy of our sacred texts has to be acknowledged. Once the Torah is no longer understood to be infallible, a perfect, unchanged and unchangeable record of the eternal divine will toward humankind, then much of what has been termed the 'fundamentalist' position falls apart. This will be discussed in more detail in the next section.

From a liberal point of view, it has been argued that only what a person undertakes to do out of free will based on autonomous, independent choice can constitute genuine and mature activity. Far from being a call to the true religious life, views such as those of Hirsch and Leibowitz quoted above present a barrier to authentic belief. How can a person accept what he or she is not free to weigh and consider? If indeed he or she is pushed into accepting it, how can this be true service of God? How can faith possibly demand suspension of judgment? The faithful automaton has no true faith at all. In religion, such an argument runs, rules are of secondary importance at most. What matters are the feelings of the heart; let a person practise what rituals he or she likes.

But there are problems with this view also. In the first place, it undervalues religious tradition and thereby undermines the basis for spiritual community together with the opportunities it offers for the individual to develop inwardly by following a tried and tested path. Whatever form of Jewish life we follow, it will be the case that it sets boundaries to the free choice of the individual, both on account of its communal nature and because of its spiritual demands. These limitations go far beyond what all civilized countries require in the name of the self-interest of the citizen and the well-being of society. Thus Judaism asks us to be active participants in communities with shared concerns and mutual obligations. Hillel's dictum 'do not separate from the community'[12] is axiomatic; Judaism has never condoned the attitude of the person who wants to 'go it alone'. Indeed there are times, such as periods of communal joy or sadness, when even the most pressing needs of the individual, such as the expression of grief at a time of bereavement, are set aside in public in favour of the mood of the group as a whole. As Esriel Hildesheimer wrote: 'The life of a religious Jew is never an autonomous one. [Judaism] is not a personal matter, closed or individual. In his thoughts, and also in his feelings of joy as well as pain, the Jew finds himself connected with the rest of his people.'[13] Equally, in the spiritual domain, traditional Judaism has never considered the question of whether or not one observes the Sabbath or the festivals, or daily prayer for that matter, as open to negotiation. These are things we have to do, times in our diary, which we are simply required to set aside whether we like it or not. Thus, if we wish to take our Judaism seriously, key factors, both social and spiritual, will limit our freedom to do what we like when we like. Indeed, if it is to be honoured in any serious manner, the requirement that we live our lives according to God's will presents us with the ultimate challenge of transforming and transcending the more selfish parts of our character, a demand which both ordinary Jews and saintly rabbis have met throughout the ages, often in the most painful of circumstances.

In the second place, we may question whether personal autonomy, albeit limited by the need to provide a similar degree of freedom to others, really is the measure of all things. The right to choose our course of action may be central to our concept of liberty, but that does not make it, in and of itself, into the supreme value. The depressing history of our century and the troubled state of modern society have made this abundantly clear. Indeed, the current return to religion and the adoption by many of more traditional, conformist ways of life are indicative of a readiness to renounce the pursuit of individualistic goals in favour of more cohesive and externally moderated values. It has been said that we live in an age in which freedom is in search of a purpose.

Where do these considerations take us? The fact is that they leave many of us facing dilemmas and trying to resolve them as best we can. Aware as we may be of the traditional view discussed above that doing precedes understanding, we will nevertheless seek to evaluate our choices, even if this is only possible to a limited extent. At this point the issue ceases to be a purely intellectual question and becomes largely a practical and personal matter as well. For the decisions we in the end make about our religious life are based upon many and varied concerns.

The personal dimension cannot be ignored: by and large we do what seems reasonably familiar in a setting that feels reasonably safe. Almost everyone wants to feel that he or she belongs. The questions are therefore: Am I comfortable in this or in that community, with this or with that kind of Jewish life? Will I be judged and marginalized, or accepted and included? Is there a place here for my family? Am I likely to make friends? Yet the issues of values and principles remain: Am I following what I genuinely believe to be true? Am I striving hard enough, indeed am I being encouraged strongly enough, to do what is right? Is this Judaism helping me to do good, both within my own community and for the wider society? Does it sharpen or dull the conscience? Not least are the spiritual concerns: Does this way of life make me more aware that I have a soul, or is it merely a form of religious behaviourism? Has it the capacity to purify my life? Will it be able to help me in the crises of my years, facing bereavements and my own death? Perhaps most significantly of all, there will be questions of authenticity: Am I being true to myself? Am I being true to the religion of my parents and grandparents? Is this what I believe I ought to be doing?

For many who struggle with these matters there is a further concern about the kind of Judaism one seeks to provide for one's children. How one chooses for them may well determine the choices one makes for oneself. Indeed it is often the challenge of giving their children the Jewish life they want them to have that leads parents to do more for themselves. Children will of course have to confront their own dilemmas, but can one at least help them to do so out of knowledge rather than from ignorance? Can we give them advantages we ourselves did not have? Those who take such questions seriously will be aware that the critical factor here is not just the school to which the children are sent but the example we ourselves set. Little is more absurd than the notion that the parent, or the adult group in general, should show the child a little of everything so that the latter may be allowed to make his or her own unbiased decisions on the threshold of maturity.

The huge responsibility of parenthood cannot be fulfilled by default. How, ideally, should we seek to bear it? We would wish to influence our children for good from birth, to nurture them in their tradition through the food they eat, the smells from the kitchen, the sounds they hear, the sights they see and the activities they engage in. We would not do this in a spirit of cynical manipulation. We would seek to convey to them that our Judaism forms the basis and the fabric of our life, that it gives us our moral values, our spiritual inspiration and discipline, and that we love it and desire to pass on that love to them as their portion and their heritage. We would seek the affection and assent of their spirit, not just their dull obedience (though the latter would doubtless have to be exacted from them in times of lesser motivation!). But at the same time we would teach them to question and to challenge and that there are many valid ways of living an authentic Jewish life. In this way, we would hope that Judaism would become so deeply rooted in them that even in the periods when they feel lost it will not cease to grow in ways unseen. Then, we trust, they will turn to the Torah and discover it, freely and willingly, for themselves.

5. Torah from Heaven

A concept which cannot be ignored when considering the question of the authority of Judaism and Jewish law is that of *Torah min Hashamayim*, Torah from Heaven. The words are extremely emotive; in recent times they have unfortunately become *the* slogan in the frequently acrimonious theological debate over the origins of Torah. The confrontation between 'fundamentalists' and 'non-fundamentalists', between those who take the words 'Torah from Heaven' to mean that God literally dictated every word of the written Torah and those who do not, cannot be dismissed. Its consequences for the future development of both Jewish theology and Jewish society are enormous. Nevertheless, it is my contention that the present focus on them, caused largely by the way in which they have been hijacked in defence of orthodoxy, detracts from the real significance of the words *Torah Min Hashamayim* and prevents us from learning from them. For what they actually express is the principle of unity within continuity, the ability of a tradition to remain bound to its core and its central text, while at the same time fostering creativity and exploration. The real importance of *Torah min Hashamayim* is to be discovered in the way in which we negotiate change and new ideas, not in the way we seek to maintain fixity.

To return to the current debate, there are those who hold that

the words 'Torah from Heaven' have one and only one meaning: God gave the Torah to His people Israel verse by verse and
word by word in more or less exactly the form in which we have
it today. Every sentence, every idea, every law is therefore the
Word of God, and no human being is at liberty to change or
amend or deny the significance of anything in the text. The
Torah commands our obedience because it is the expression of
God's will as God dictated it through Moses to us. This was the
view of Maimonides, Joseph Caro, author of the *Shulchan
Aruch*, and almost all of the sages since their times, and it
remains the view of orthodox leadership today. Indeed, orthodoxy is often defined in relationship to this position. It would be
wrong, however, to ascribe to all who hold it the inflexible
attitude of 'ours not to question why, ours but to do or die'.
Maimonides was, for example, a leading proponent of the view
that we can and should attempt to understand the reasons for
the commandments, although we must obey them whatever the
results of our enquiries. It would also be wrong to ascribe to all
orthodox thinkers the extreme view of the Chatam Sofer, Rabbi
Moses Sofer of Pressburg, who declared that 'everything new is
forbidden according to the Torah'.[14] This statement, in fact a
Mishnah in which the word *chadash*, or new, has a technical
meaning, was transformed into a battle cry in which *chadash*
came to mean anything newfangled, and was used in the early
nineteenth century as an attack on reforming activity. It was,
therefore, the counter-offensive of a leader who correctly perceived the world of traditional Judaism to be under threat and
who responded forcefully. That Jewish law, the oral Torah, has
developed, that it has not been held still through the ages in
some divinely mandated hypostasis, is a fact accepted to greater
or lesser degree by almost all rabbis. But that the written Torah
may itself have a history is an idea which has proved problematic, to say the least, to the defenders of traditional orthodoxy.

Other thinkers, notably in this country Rabbi Louis Jacobs,
have found it impossible to uphold so literal an interpretation of

the concept of Torah from Heaven. An awareness of history, the study in that light of the text of the Torah itself, the greater knowledge of the law and literature of surrounding nations, all suggest that the Torah was written in the context and under the influence of its times. The argument that we should suspend our judgment when it comes to the Torah and not apply to it the same methods of analysis which we adopt in approaching other texts is far from compelling. On the contrary, it would surely be unworthy to seek to serve God other than with complete integrity and in truth, hence with every tool of knowledge at our disposal. Thus there are many who believe that Judaism, including both the written Torah and the oral Torah, has developed in an historical context and through human mediation. Torah is indeed the expression of the Divine will, but the Divine will as manifest through human comprehension, a comprehension pushed to but nevertheless within its own ultimate limitations and those of the times. The Torah is seen, therefore, as 'from Heaven', not in the sense that it dropped from Heaven, but in the sense that it is inspired from, and is thus based on, our relationship with Heaven. But it takes the physical form it does because God's revelation and guidance are filtered through the human mind and articulated within the context of the society, laws and history of the times.

A consequence of this position is that the injunctions of the Torah can no longer be regarded simply as unquestionable and eternal verities. To many this is a liberating thought: how, after all, could anyone have imagined that the existence of slaves could be tolerable in the eyes of God, that we are to wage an eternal war against the nation of the Amalekites, however evil the actions of the latter; that the rebellious child who failed to heed due warnings was to be stoned, or that women were to suffer for ever from the demeaning disadvantages to which, in various circumstances, the Torah condemns them? Does it not make far more sense to see these matters as the product of what people at that time considered the will of God to be? Did not the rabbis themselves, throughout the classic period of the Mishnah and the Talmud, find ways of disagreeing with and of voiding – while maintaining the concept of the infallibility of the Torah – such legislation of all relevance and all bite? And they too were, inevitably, the prisoners of their time. For we see things differently from how they did, finding certain, though relatively few, aspects of rabbinic law difficult to accept morally. And future generations will look at us with equally critical eyes. Yet everything is still 'Torah from Heaven' because it derives from the same initial process of revelation and is related back to the same core text and belongs within the same tradition of interpretation.

To others this 'non-fundamentalist' position is abhorrent and threatening. It undermines the whole fabric of Judaism. For if we deny that every word of the Torah is literally the word of God, then we remove the absolute divine authority from Torah. Without such authority what will become of it? Who will keep it any more? It is a total betrayal not only of Jewish belief but also of Jewish history to do such a thing.

Yet, however disturbing that claim may be, it must be noted that it is an argument about effectiveness, not one about truth. To the question of truth it is absolutely irrelevant. Still, it might perhaps be maintained, is not effectiveness more important than truth? If a good thing will be done if we say that it is absolutely and literally the word of God, is not that what we should be saying? But there is something dubious about such a challenge: the argument which makes integrity subject to utility, and which bases itself on grounds of power and effectiveness, must always be suspect in the end. Of course, there are occasions in every field of activity when it is not the time to ask why, when things have to be done, habits consolidated and no risks taken. But in the end issues of truth cannot be suppressed, except at a terrible price.

Imposed in the form of absolute dogmas which may not be challenged, religious authority carries the same distasteful impli-

cations as any other form of absolute power. A world full of
religions, each claiming total and unquestionable knowledge of
the truth, would be little different from a playground full of
children all crying 'me, me, me'. This is not an attitude Judaism
has countenanced, welcoming as it does the truth from
wherever it may come, and holding as it does that the faculty of
reason and the intuitions of the heart are gifts of God. The
authority of Torah rests in its Divine inspiration, on the long
history of meditation upon it and analysis of it, and on the
intrinsic value of the traditional Jewish practices that have
emerged from that process. This authority is best maintained
through firm and consistent, but open and questioning, education in the context of Judaism lived and loved, and is best
supported by the faith that most human beings, thus directed,
ultimately seek the true and the good.

All this should certainly not, however, be taken to mean that
the concept of Torah from Heaven is meaningless to one who
holds a non-literalist position. Those who do so would say
that *Torah min Hashamayim*, as a belief in the uninterrupted
chain of inspiration the ultimate source of which is the revelation of the Divine will, and which has been mediated by many
tens of generations of interpretation by the most sensitized
spirits and the most refined minds, is a *sine qua non* of Judaism.
The great works of our tradition simply cannot be understood
other than in the light of this belief, which has made of every
letter of the Torah a significant vehicle for the revelation of
God's presence. A person who invariably dons his or her
critical spectacles before examining every text or committing
themselves to any action will almost certainly remain ignorant
of the deeper spirit of our traditions. One would say further
that the laws and statutes and customs which form the daily,
weekly and yearly practices of Judaism are to be trusted and
followed and that a person who in no way does so can have
little appreciation of their power to foster the spiritual life or
of the wisdom which engendered them. But this is a vastly

different position from that of those who maintain that it is wrong to take a critical approach towards anything we find in the Torah, and that there are areas in which enquiry must be outlawed. Did not the Rabbis of the Talmud themselves render certain laws a dead letter, using only the pretext that the Torah had never intended them to be carried out? Has Judaism ever stood still?

On the contrary, the significance of Torah from Heaven can best be understood within the context of change. It expresses the principle of unity and continuity in a tradition that has constantly been subject to further exploration and thorough re-examination. The Talmud tells the story of how God transports Moses to the academy of Rabbi Akiva. There he sits in the back row and cannot understand a word. When, however, he is assured that this is Torah, the same Torah which at this moment in time God is preparing to give through him to the people of Israel, Moses is satisfied.[15] The Torah has developed beyond recognition, but it is the Torah nonetheless. The significance of the story is twofold. In the first place, once the Torah has been given to human beings, it is, in its own words, 'not in heaven'. It is subject to human interpretation and the decisive factor is not prayerful appeal to God but the acumen of human judgment and the ability to respond to the demands of changing situations. Secondly, the story expresses the confidence that human beings can and will use their powers of reasoning and judgment in a manner which is faithful to the intentions of the Torah in so far as these can be understood and interpreted. In other words we must have faith in the resilience of Torah and the organic vitality of Judaism.

6. *The contribution of our time*

The story is told among the Hasidim of how Rabbi Lipman of Radomsk, son-in-law of Rabbi Shlomo of Radomsk, once visited Rabbi Menachem Mendel of Kotsk. '"Tell me a teaching of your father-in-law," requested the host. "The Torah teaches us," responded the guest, "that when his two sons were killed Aaron remained silent" (Leviticus 10:3). This, my father-in-law used to say, shows a very high spiritual level. But when King David said: "That Your Glory may sing of You and not be silent" (Psalm 30.13), that was an even higher level".[16]

The whole of Jewish history can be interpreted as a dialectic between these two responses, between silence and new song. Troubles come, there is a time of silence. But soon new songs, new ideas emerge out of destruction. Time passes; for whatever reason, the innovative spirit of earlier ages falls silent. Needs arise, fresh troubles come; existential necessity proves once again to be the mother of spiritual invention and new songs are sung, new interpretations created to answer the challenges of the time. Silence is followed by sound; on the tree of life winter is followed by a season of new growth. That has been the pattern in ages past, the form of the dialogue between eternal truths and time, and it must continue in the future.

It is this approach which has allowed the Torah to be interpreted in such radically different ways. The rabbis of the Midrash, for example, may read a verse in a certain manner, connecting it with a passage dozens of chapters apart in the Bible on the basis of some apparently trivial verbal similarity; the Hasidic masters may read it totally differently, completely ignoring both syntax and context, to produce the message they desire to derive. But it is the same Torah to which they both refer. Both would hold that their meaning was implicit in the verse from before time anyway, that all they have done is to extract the essence that is already there. Yet both create a new and vital style of exegesis, both develop a fresh and timely form of dialogue with Torah. Thus throughout Jewish history, whenever there has been something to say, it has always been possible to say it by reference to Torah. In this way century after century of interpretation has embraced the Torah, surrounding it as the layers of an onion encircle the centre. Approaches have frequently been nothing less than revolutionary. Every age has responded to Torah in the light of the prevailing disciplines and concerns of its times; none has failed to find sufficient warrant for doing so in the text itself. Each new attempt at explanation, so long as it is made 'for the sake of Heaven' and in faithful love of its teachings, affirms the vitality of Torah from Heaven. Each new layer takes account both of the centre and of previous layers, adding to a tradition which is vital and whole.

The danger for us lies not in exploration but in ceasing to explore. It is in the notion that Judaism and Torah cannot cope with our doubts, questions and concerns, our insights, ideas and inspirations, that there is lack of faith. The questions of our time are the silence before our song. Only if we fail to engage with Torah in a genuine spirit, through laziness, arrogance or cowardice, will there be no song. Then we will have failed not only the tradition but also the silence.

What will the contribution of our age be to the interpretation of Torah? It would be a foolhardy person indeed who attempted to give a definitive answer. It has been said that one has to wait at least a hundred years to gain sufficient perspective on one's own place in history, a privilege with which scarcely anyone is blessed. Nevertheless, there is value in asking what the special features of our relationship with Torah may be, now, in this difficult period at the end of the twentieth century. Despite Ecclesiastes' claim that 'there is nothing new under the sun' (Eccles.1.9) and in spite of the fact that it would be hard to think of a single subject to which no helpful references can be found in our sources, there are nonetheless certain dilemmas in every age which become pressing, inescapable concerns. These have to be addressed in the language and according to the requirements of the hour. The alternative is a religion which fails to say anything about those issues which most engage the conscience of the time.

What then are our concerns? Clearly, they are influenced by

the fact that we are the generations of the Holocaust and its aftermath. Who can descend to the depths of human suffering, and who can abide in that pitiful place? Who can estimate the extent of the shock caused by that event which has its grip on us even now, fifty years later, and which has shaken the minds of all thinking people? The belief in progress that sustained much of the Western world since the Enlightenment has largely gone. Indeed, it is not only our confidence in human achievements, but our faith in human beings, in ourselves, which is broken. The idea, once widely held, that advances in knowledge and technological ability would go hand in hand with moral development is now perceived to be a fiction. If man is master of all things, he is so at his peril. At the end of the twentieth century we are less awed by what we are able to do than dismayed by what we have done, and are doing, to the world. We look at it with renewed fear; prosperity is proving no cure for insecurity. We watch ourselves poison our environment, literally and metaphorically, through war, hatred, wanton behaviour and waste. Few only rise up to do anything about it. Large numbers of people feel helpless, disillusioned, rootless and lonely. Others don't appear to care. Can Judaism address groups and issues like these? Can it afford not to?

What responses do we find? On the one hand, we experience the need to mourn for the past, to co-exist with its shadows and to draw its vanished life into our present. One lives, as it were, for two people, for oneself and for a life that was destroyed. This is a great responsibility to bear and it leads us to seek to recover and redeem Torah from the abyss into which it almost fell. There is a natural conservatism, a desire to turn round, to re-evaluate negatively the effect of the Enlightenment upon Jewish life and its achievements for all. There is a general perception that in tradition lies safety; the clock must be turned back and the doors closed on the alien outside world. This is one of the reasons for the re-emerging strength of religious orthodoxy. There is a desire to fan the embers of the spiritual fires that once burnt fiercely in the soul of the Jews of Eastern Europe, particularly among the Hasidim, and to revive the flames before it is too late. We are witnesses to a process of rediscovery and regeneration.

On the other hand there is a need for a new kind of dialogue, a contemporary medium of expression for the integration of Torah and life. It would be dangerous, a kind of retreat, if our only response to present dilemmas were little more than a repetition of old accommodations. We would be failing to confront not only the essential questions of the times but also the vital challenge of Torah. Furthermore, there is today a large new group of people who cannot be addressed, who refuse to be addressed in that way. The pious affirmations of an age-old liturgy, beloved by many, may convey to them little more than a sense of irrelevance on the one hand and of estrangement on the other. Ignorance is partly to blame. The pattern of generations, in which parents initiated their children into prayers and rituals, where synagogue was simply home from home, has been broken. Many people would love to belong as their grandparents or great-grandparents belonged, but they can't. But there are also other, and deeper, reasons for their sense of alienation. The language of the traditional synagogue, replete with certainties and frequently full of blame for those who do not or cannot uphold them, has little in common with the tentative and self-doubting testaments that form so significant a part of the discourse of many contemporary seekers. Included in the latter should be the writings of survivors, the listening of counsellor and therapist, the silence of those who will not or cannot talk. This is a literature that comprises the views, the consciousness, of all those who can subjugate themselves to no preconceived pattern, who bring tension to tradition, who challenge its values and require that it address them also. It encompasses, emphasizes even, Primo Levi's radical re-reading of the Shema, for which it has as much sympathy as the original sequence of injunctions:

Consider if this is a man
Who works in the mud
Who does not know peace
Who fights for a scrap of bread
Who dies because of a yes or a no....

Meditate that this came about:
I commend these words to you.
Carve them in your hearts
At home, in the street,
Going to bed, rising;
Repeat them to your children ...[17]

Such people and their questions, we and our questions, have to be addressed. It is not enough simply to aspire to go back to the habits of the past. Return must include re-evaluation. Otherwise there will be repetition, but no renewal. We may be encouraged or cajoled into observing the commandments, but we will express no sense of values adequate to the challenges of our time through our observance. The contribution of our age to the interpretation of Torah must lie in the results of allowing the two languages, tradition and testament, that of the rooted and that of the rootless, to meet. Our commentaries may well be more personal than those of previous ages; they may contain many stories and express their truths in instances from biographies rather than in abstract beliefs. Yet these matters have to be given their place, and we must have confidence in the ability of Torah and life to speak to one another.

This is not a confrontation essentially different in kind from that which must have followed the crushing of Judaea by the Romans in the first century and the defeat of the Bar Kochba revolt in the middle of the second, or than that which must have been occasioned by the destruction and dispersion of the communities of Spain in the fifteenth. As then, so now, it is a challenge to be faced by the community as a whole. Those who experience themselves as addressed by it, and whose existential unease motivates them to write about and teach Torah, cannot be separated from those who choose not to do so along the old battle lines of Orthodox against Liberal. This issue unites those whom other scores have divided. Thus Lionel Blue, a British Reform Rabbi, can write that 'in the last few years, my renewal has come from retreats which I have "conducted" for the terminally ill, alcoholics, HIV carriers, and AIDS sufferers. I have put "conducted" in inverted commas, because the retreatants conducted me back to belief, and goodness ... They led me back to spirituality and love of life beyond the body and to what grows out of disintegration. The sources of my religion and strength are marginalized, suffering people.'[18] At the same time Joseph Dov Soloveitchik, the spokesman for a generation of American orthodoxy, can say in *The Lonely Man Of Faith*: 'All I want is to follow the advice given by Elihu, the son of Berachel of old, who said, "I will speak that I may find relief"; for there is a redemptive quality for an agitated mind in the spoken word, and a tormented soul finds peace in confessing ...What can a man of faith like myself, living by a doctrine which has no technical potential, by a law which cannot be tested in any laboratory, steadfast in his loyalty to an eschatological vision whose fulfilment cannot be predicted with any degree of probability, let alone certainty ... what can such a man say to a functional, utilitarian society which is saeculum-oriented and whose practical reasons of the mind have long ago supplanted the sensitive reasons of the heart?'[19]

In tension is life; in challenge the relevance of Torah is revealed. If we do not bring to it the issues of our conscience and our day, we and our Judaism will live impoverished and bifurcating lives. But such a meeting, though no one can predict precisely how, will, I believe, reaffirm the vitality of Torah just as previous generations have affirmed it. For out of the silence the Torah will inspire us to sing to our God a new song.

III

Gemilut Hasadim – Acts of Faithful Love

The diameter of the explosion was thirty centimetres
and the diameter of the area affected approximately seven
meters
in which there were four killed and eleven wounded.
Around these, in a greater circle
of pain and time, were scattered two hospitals
and one cemetery. But the young woman
who was buried in the place she had come from,
a distance of over a hundred kilometres,
made the circle very much larger indeed,
and the lonely man weeping over her death
in the shires of some distant country across the seas
caused the whole world to be included in the circle ...

(Yehudah Amichai)[1]

1. Great is learning, for learning leads to action

'Deeds speak louder than words,' runs the familiar saying. The
rabbis of the Talmud would probably have agreed, although
they saw the matter somewhat differently. To them, deeds were
the fruit of words, the end and aim of the study of the words of
Torah in particular. Thus, in the hotly debated argument as to
which is greater, learning or action, victory is accorded neither
to theory nor to practice alone. Instead, the discussion results
in a compromise which has justifiably become famous: 'great
is learning for learning leads to action'.[2] Action without

71

knowledge leads nowhere; it is little more than undirected energy. Learning which does not result in action is an indulgence: to know what is right but not to do it is a double wrong. Important as our relationship with God is, it cannot be maintained at the expense of our responsibilities in this world. At the end of our study we must turn back to our duties with a renewed sense of moral commitment. At the conclusion of our prayers we are to resume our tasks reinvigorated and inspired. For we are here in this world to do: it is a serious misunderstanding of the purpose of study and prayer if we regard them as alternatives, if they lead us to imagine that God will act on our behalf. We have no right to make such assumptions or permit ourselves such evasions. On the contrary, Torah and Tefillah should sensitize our conscience, sharpen our moral awareness, lead us into war with our own complacency. Deeds, well considered and directed, must be the result. This is the meaning of *gemilut hasadim,* acts of faithful love. It is our response to our responsibilities, it is what we do with the energy and will, with the love and the indignation that our life and learning arouse within us.

Judaism is thus no quietist religion. The needs of others are our necessary concern and the issues of our society are our issues. Our prophets, rabbis and leaders have not lived in splendid isolation from, but rather in intimate association with, those around them. In bonds of love, but also in bitter social satire and in political diatribe, they have bound themselves to the people and involved themselves in the moral confrontations of their times. By no means, either, is this to be seen as the responsibility of the great or the prerogative of the famous. We do not have to be prophets or scholars. Each in our own way and each according to our particular capacities, Judaism asks us to make our commitments to what is good and right. Of course, nobody can be expected to become involved in everything, and there are very real limits to what we can achieve; but if, in the words of Rabbi Tarfon, it is not our duty to complete the work, neither are we free to desist from it.[3]

Gemilut Hasadim – Acts of Faithful Love

In the previous chapters of this book the focus was mainly on the vertical relationship, between ourselves and God; here it will be chiefly on the horizontal dimension, the connection between ourselves and other people. Nevertheless, *gemilut hasadim* will not be seen as entirely earth-centred; it will be considered in the context of the vocabulary and tradition to which it belongs. What is the effect of our behaviour towards other people on our relationship with God, and what does our relationship with God require of us in our conduct towards other people? What is God's responsibility and what ours? It is in the context of this connection between heaven and earth that I want to examine the sense of interconnectedness, of solidarity in fact, which the concept of *gemilut hesed* really implies. What demands does the principle of acts of faithful love make on us in our relationships with those close to us, with our community and with our society at large? What is the furthest diameter of the effect of our deeds? Do we have to be concerned with what happens far away, or are such things beyond the bounds of our moral responsibility? What, above all, must there be at the centre of the circle, in our hearts and minds, if we are to be able to respond? What demands does the need to be there with and for others make on our understanding of ourselves? What does being Jewish mean to us and what does Judaism require of us in each of these spheres of interaction?

There can be no doubt that these issues trouble us deeply. When Keats wrote his sonnet 'To Sleep', he asked that 'soft embalmer of the still midnight' to save him 'from curious Conscience, that still lords / Its strength for darkness'. For often one lies awake at night, the conscience irritated into unease by some little remark, some passing, throw-away comment which now one regrets. But as one thinks, as the minutes become hours and as one takes to heart the fact that this 'little thing' will not leave one alone, one begins to realize that it had, perhaps, further dimensions unrecognized before. 'I hurt him, I must have really hurt him,' one says to oneself in the end, 'and

73

who knows how far the hurt has carried by this time?' Then, perhaps, one tries to re-run the scene, going over it ten times more to convince oneself that everything was really all right. But the effort is in vain; it will not leave one alone. It is done; it cannot be retracted.

For good or for bad the effect of our actions spreads out around us in ever-expanding circles like the ripples set in motion by throwing a stone into a pond. Once started they cannot be stopped. None of us can totally undo what we have done; other actions take their place perhaps, trust is rebuilt, or broken down, but our deeds have gone out into the world and cannot retroactively be withdrawn. *Gemilut hasadim* therefore represents a practical value intended to inculcate in us good habits in all our dealings. It begins at home, but it does not end there. It extends in a widening radius around us, including our family and friends, our community, members of other communities, groups and peoples whom we may never know or even see, our environment itself. According to the Talmud, it belongs to that category of actions which has no limits, like the study of Torah.[4] It impacts on every area of life.

Furthermore, *Gemilut Hesed* has a double role: it is both proactive and reactive. In the first case, it is the guiding principle in all our relationships with other people, a positive attitude that we seek to develop in ourselves and to inculcate into our children to the point where it becomes a natural habit of basic kindness and trustworthiness in all our ways. As such it is a quality which cannot be overestimated. A friend once told me that when his father was on his deathbed he had asked him what he should look for in the girl he was to marry. 'She should be kind,' was the answer, 'all the rest is secondary.'

In the second case, *Gemilut Hesed* is the approach by means of which we strive to counteract the cruelty, pain and loneliness with which the world is filled. As acts of wanton destruction engulf more and more of our human and natural environment, so we must struggle ever harder to respond in a way which can bring healing and restoration. The only cure for groundless hate, our rabbis teach, is selfless love. *Gemilut Hesed* is thus more than an attitude or attribute, a characteristic found in lesser measure in some and in greater measure in others. It is an approach to life. As such it has a specifically religious significance, devolving from the nature of the relationship between God and the creation. What then is the context of *Gemilut Hesed*?

2. *Our response to our responsibility*

Gemilut hasadim is the sort of phrase which it is notoriously difficult to translate. A literal rendition, such for example as 'acts of loving kindness', may not be inaccurate; in the Bible *hesed* is indeed used to describe kindness and goodness towards other people in general as well as to indicate a merciful attitude to those in need in particular. But such a translation fails to convey the significance of the words in the context of the relationship between God and human beings, as part of a specifically religious vocabulary. For *gemilut hasadim* indicates not only natural, gratuitous acts of kindness but more particularly the love and mercy which partners in a covenant are expected to show to one another. We and God are such partners; the *hesed* we do, or do not, show to one another points to the loving fidelity which can and should exist between us. Thus Abraham, God's partner in the first such covenant, the pact with which the Jewish people begins, is renowned for his *hesed*, his concern for others and his devoted loyalty. God's promise to Abraham's descendants, given as a response to Abraham's fidelity, is that the Divine *hesed* will never depart from them. Hence, throughout the tribulations of our history, whenever the fear of abandonment has threatened to flood our hearts, we turn to God and pray that the Divine attribute of *hesed*, and not judgment, should be to the fore. Equally, when God sees the people departing from the right way, the prophet is sent to remind them: 'Thus saith the Lord; I remember unto you the faithful kindness of your youth, the love of your bridal days, when you followed after me through the wilderness, through an unsown land' (Jer. 2.2).

As a value, *hesed* does not stand alone. Most often it is compared to *tzedakah*, a word generally translated as 'charity' but which, as its root indicates, might better be rendered as 'righteousness' or 'right action'. This removes the inappropriate connotation of worthy benevolence and points to the real significance of *tzedakah* as the expression of a commitment to what is just and fair. Nevertheless, *gemilut hasadim* remains greater than *tzedakah*. The relationship between them is one of inclusion; the former comprises but is more than the latter. 'Our rabbis taught: in three ways *gemilut hesed* is greater than *tzedakah. Tzedakah* is performed with money; *gemilut hesed* both with money and with personal action. *Tzedakah* is for the poor; *gemilut hesed* both for the poor and for the rich. *Tzedakah* is for the living; *gemilut hesed* both for the living and the dead.'[5] But it would be wrong to diminish the importance of *tzedakah;* the readiness to share what is ours and to give generously because that is our responsibility is something on which the Jewish community has rightly prided itself. Our rabbis even set measures for how much one should give, twenty per cent being the upper limit, ten per cent average and five per cent of one's income the mean minimum. But *gemilut hasadim* is greater because it involves the self, not only the purse.

More fundamental is the connection between *gemilut hesed* and the word which more than any other points to the nature of our relationship with God, *emunah* or faith. The two belong closely together. If *emunah* expresses the relationship between people and God as a whole, then *gemilut hesed* is the positive manifestation of it in acts which both affirm and help to create it. When love falters, faith experiences a moment of failure; where love and devotion are found, there faith is fostered and restored. *Gemilut hesed* is loyal behaviour in the context of the relationship of faith. It is for this reason that I have chosen to translate it as 'acts of faithful love'. Such conduct is part of our commitment to a partnership with God which demands of us not only that we study and pray, but also that we dedicate ourselves to life by giving with heart and mind and hand, with time and effort and fortune. These things are what we owe in return for the privilege of living in God's world, however harsh and hopeless life there may sometimes seem. They represent our part in the mutual task of *tikkun olam,* the betterment of the world. God, so Judaism teaches, will bring the redemption at the end of days. That, however, is not our central concern. Our chief duty is to play our part, and we do so by means of *gemilut hesed*. This is no mere gratuitous act of goodness on our part; it is the fulfilment of a covenant, our response to our responsibility.

3. *God's responsibility, or ours?*

According to the Zohar, when Noah opened the door of the ark and saw the devastation caused by the flood, a land of stumps, of broken trees and carcasses of animals, he wept. God said to him then: 'It's all very well weeping now, but did you have to save your tears till after it was all too late? Where were you when there was still time?' The comment has, of course, a frightening and painful relevance to a generation which, watching itself destroy its planet, for the most part indulges its own indifference, or destructiveness, or greed. But in Noah's case was God's criticism fair? After all, it wasn't he who brought the flood. How could God, who caused it, blame Noah for weeping over its effects? Even if we accept that the real reason for the inundation was the sinfulness of the generation which it came to punish, was Noah to blame for what happened? Or was God, perhaps, upset with Noah because He was also upset with Himself, angry with him for shedding tears too late, because He also, as it were, was weeping afterwards?

The answer traditionally given is that Noah was guilty of

indifference: he got into his ark and did nothing to avert the fate of the rest of humankind. He should have argued, both with man and with God, reproving the thoughtless conduct of the former and the destructive anger of the latter. He should have cared more, cared more even than his Creator. What God's responsibility was and is remains an intractable problem, 'the secret things belong to the Lord' (Deut. 29.25). But our responsibilities lie before us, immediate and commanding.

Abraham understood what his ancestor had not. This becomes clear if we ask the question: Why Abraham? The answer does not emerge immediately. When God first speaks to him saying *'lech lecha* – get thee gone from thy land, from thy mother country, from the house of thy father' (Gen. 12.1) the Torah gives no reason why, out of the long passage of time, out of all the possible people who had been alive and died since Noah, God should have chosen him. On this crucial point the text remains silent. But the rabbis of the Midrash, and the interpreters and homilists who followed in their wake, found answers: Abraham was the first to discover the true God; Abraham realized the world had an owner and Creator; Abraham understood that there was a reason why a terrible fate overtook the wicked ... Be all that as it may, the Torah which was silent at the moment of Abraham's first call is not so afterwards. For when God determines to destroy the town of Sodom and the cities of the plain, He first informs Abraham, making His reasons for doing so abundantly clear: 'For I have known him, to the end that he may command his children and his household after him, that they may keep the way of the Lord, to do righteousness and justice' (Gen. 18.19). 'I have known him' tells us that between God and Abraham there exists a close and continuing relationship. 'To the end that' indicates that this contact between them has a purpose to which they are both bound. 'To do righteousness and justice' explains what the objective is for the sake of which they are bound to one another in mutual responsibility. Thus God tells Abraham of the planned destruction of the cities of the plain not in spite of, but precisely because of, the fact that He knows the man will argue. That he cares enough, both about his fellow humans and about God, to do so is part of the Torah's answer to the question 'Why Abraham?'

But the challenge which Abraham issues is no less disturbing than it is elevating. For it is no small thing to accuse the final arbiter of right and wrong of being heedless and unfair. 'How can you do this?' Abraham cries out, 'How can you destroy the righteous and the wicked alike?' 'Shall the judge of all the earth not do justly?' (Gen. 18.25). The Midrash seizes upon the subversive potential of his challenge: 'Rabbi Shmuel ben Nachman said: [God's decision to inform Abraham before the destruction of Sodom and Gomorrah] may be compared to the case of a king who had an adviser without whose consent he did nothing. On one occasion, however, he wished to do something without his agreement, whereupon he observed: "Surely I made him my adviser for no other reason than that I should do nothing without his consent."'[6] Abraham's moral authority is thus presented as greater even than that of God. The reader is asked to consider the disturbing thought that the true guardian of justice may not be God but humanity. Yet, or so at least the Midrash gives us to understand, that is the case because God wishes it to be thus. God willingly entrusts the responsibility for justice and compassionate concern to Abraham, and through him to all humankind. God had made pacts before then (with Noah after the flood), and would do so afterwards (with the children of Israel at Sinai), but the true history of the covenant really begins here, with Abraham. '*Titten ... hesed le'Avraham*', the prophet says: 'You gave the quality of faithful love to Abraham' (Micah 7.20). The love referred to is more than theoretical justice; it is a love based on the knowledge of what it is to be human, coupled with an understanding of the responsibility of partnership with God. The custodianship of *hesed* You, God, have delegated to us.

This message was brought home to me when I first read as an adult a story written by my mother. It concerns a young boy who sets out from home to search for the right way to walk in life. Eventually he meets an old man who, to his great surprise, tells him that he knows the boy's parents, and his grandparents, indeed the whole of his family. Startled by this strange coincidence the boy looks hard at the old man and at length recognizes in the venerable stranger his ancestor Abraham. Now a new concern comes over him, a fresh curiosity to which he gives expression in a string of questions:

'I set out, but no voice came to tell me which way I should go. I am probably not worthy of the voice. But as for you, you managed to find your way. Tell me, do tell me, how you found it.'

Abraham looked steadily at the boy but remained silent.

'You were promised a land,' the boy continued quietly, 'was it this promise which helped you find your way?'

Abraham shook his head.

'You were promised descendants, numerous as the sands of the sea; was it this promise which helped you find your way?'

Abraham shook his head and remained silent ...

... At length Abraham spoke: 'It wasn't the promise of a land nor was it the promise of descendants. I was told: Through you will all the families of the earth be blessed. I knew then that a great blessing had been placed on my shoulders. I had to bear it and it showed me the way.'

Resting his peaceful eyes on the boy and gently touching the nape of his neck, he said 'through you' ... and disappeared.[7]

4. And he said, 'Here am I' (Gen. 22.1)

When God called to him, Abraham said '*Hinneni* – Here am I'. When God asked him where his brother was, Cain said '*Lo yadati* – I don't know' (Gen. 4.9). These two simple, instinctive answers mark the opposing poles of our moral response, the one for good and the other for bad. *Gemilut hesed* is first and foremost a requirement that we say '*hinneni* – here am I', that we stand by what is good.

This applies to the whole of life; it is no less relevant in times of joy than it is in the season of sorrow; it is just as much a commandment that we rejoice with bride and bridegroom on their wedding day as it is that we should support the mourner at the side of the open grave. But it is a well known adage that plenty finds many friends while few remain to support the person who has fallen on hard times. Therefore the principle of *gemilut hesed* comes to teach us that when another person needs us, whatever the nature of the need, in poverty or in wealth, in life or at the door of death, we should be there. When someone is ill, we should be at the bedside. When someone is dying, he or she should not be abandoned to loneliness. When sorrow needs words, we should be there to listen, and when it requires the companionship of silence we should be there silently. Sometimes something more is necessary, but often being there, simple companionship, is enough.

But, as everyone well knows, this is not always as easy as it sounds. Who wants to witness another person's pain? Who wants to see and feel suffering, or to contemplate the thought that 'one day it will be me'? In our society we may not hold with the old superstition that the angel of death dances invisibly in dangerous places, but we are bound nonetheless by a great fear of being among the sick and the bereaved. Maybe it is the institutionalization of the old and the ill and all those who most remind us of our mortality that makes us so unused to confronting it and them. But that can only be a partial answer; it is as much a result as a cause. I shall never forget a conversation with a psychotherapist who specializes in working with the dying. 'Most people,' he told me, 'do not die of the disease. They die of loneliness.' They watch those around them withdraw, communicating, by look or by demeanour, the sense that there is no hope and that the victim of the illness is not worth talking to any more because there is nothing of value that can be given in either direction. Aware of his or her increasing isolation, the sick person tacitly complies with the judgment that he or she is of no further use, gives up hope and dies.[8] To say 'Hinneni' in such circumstances is difficult.

Everybody knows the famous excuse with which Cain, the first murderer, answered God's enquiry 'Where is Abel your brother?' (Gen.4.9). But the much quoted words 'Am I my brother's keeper?' are preceded by a less noted and apparently innocuous introduction, the throw-away sentence already quoted, 'I don't know'. One can almost visualize the nonchalant shrug of the shoulders with which Cain disclaims responsibility. The words deserve more attention than they have generally been given. Is there not such an 'I don't know' before every shameful act? Have we not all been guilty of saying it at one time or another? The following phrases may all be perfectly true and quite innocuous, but therein also lies their value as evasions: 'I wasn't there'; 'I don't know what you're talking about'; 'It's none of my business'; 'Surely you weren't expecting me to get involved'. Ignorance may, of course, be genuine, but it is often less than innocent. After all, very few children find it impossible to contrive, and this is not an ability we lose entirely when we become adults. A certain semi-conscious 'I don't want to know, so I'm not going to know' has influenced the attentiveness of the human gaze ever since the time of Cain. After all, one can, as we all know, be living next door and yet 'have no idea' what fate overtook one's neighbours in the night. Even ordinary people like ourselves are liable to cross the road or change the subject to avoid what we are too frightened to confront. There are many things of which we are indeed ignorant, and there have been many concerning which to be anything other than ignorant is far too dangerous to contemplate. But the risk is that 'I don't know' and especially 'I don't want to know' often become the prelude to 'I don't care'. Significantly, in the Bible the word used by Cain means not only 'to know' in an intellectual sense but also, in certain contexts, 'to have a relationship with', even 'to be mutually responsible towards', 'to empathize' or 'to be at one with'. Not to know is thus to disclaim responsibility and to abrogate the trust invested in human fellowship. To avert the gaze is therefore the first small step, the initial disavowal, at the beginning of the path towards betrayal. The Torah does not permit such conduct. It will not allow us to deny responsibility, even when we see a lost or fallen animal, be it indeed the possession of our worst enemy. 'You may not hide yourself away', it says, we may not pretend we didn't notice (Deut. 22.3). How much more so, then, where people, our own fellow human beings, are concerned: we may not pretend that we do not know.

The opposite of 'I don't know' is the simple word *'Hinneni* – here am I'. We too must be ready to say that word, with which the people in the Bible so often respond to the voice of God. Rashi explains *'Hinneni'* to be an expression of readiness and of humility (see his commentary on Gen.22.1). Of course, nobody can say *'Hinneni'* all the time. But it is our responsibility to say it some of the time and to strive, when need is right there before us, not to default and not to betray. Our abilities and our particular sensitivities differ; none of us can be there for everyone or everything. It is up to us to choose one or two particular areas of life in which to make our contribution, but then we must go ahead and try to make it. What life can there be if we live it without ever saying *'Hinneni'*?

Yet being there is hard. There are, of course, many ways in which *gemilut hesed* can – and even should – be conducted at a distance. From time to time voices are raised in condemnation of the 'cheque book givers' for not giving of themselves. But there is a time and place for everything; thousands of organizations depend on such support, which in fact makes it possible for others to give more personally. To give money is not simply a privilege; it is an obligation and indeed a right. A poor person is not to be denied the opportunity of making a financial contribution. Giving is one of the ways by which we experience ourselves as being of worth, a legitimate feeling so long as it doesn't take on pompous and ugly proportions. Some people give through doing, by loading lorries with food to be sent to cities under siege; some by teaching strangers in a new land the language of their place of refuge; some by taking meals on wheels to the housebound. All these constitute 'giving with one's person', and, not least, with one's time. Yet there remains something else, something deeper at the core of it all: the readiness, where appropriate, to be there oneself. Of course, this may not be what is required; money, food, clothing and skills are often what is really wanted. Furthermore, people often need their privacy, and nobody appreciates an invasion of their space, however well intended. But it remains true that there are times in all of our lives when what is asked of us is simply to be present. On such occasions being busy, fussing about externals and restlessly asking what one can do next is not helpful. It is the human being in us that is required, free of the trammels of outer preoccupations, free of prejudices and evasions.

5. Facing our own flesh

Some years ago there was a short series of radio programmes on the subject of courage. In one of them the presenter interviewed a young man who had twice been very ill and close to death. He was asked what had most helped him to pull through. Medical care had been good, he answered, but even better had been the human contact of those nurses or doctors who had stopped by the bed to talk to him and to hold his hand. It was the closeness and genuineness of the communication that had mattered most. I was myself recently at the bedside of a man whose death was clearly imminent. He could no longer talk but was able to communicate a little by means of small gestures with his fingers. At the invitation of the family I sat down next to the bed and held the old man's hand. After a minute or two spent silently in this fashion I found myself becoming more and more embarrassed. I felt that I was contributing nothing to either the family or the patient and was simply in the way. But when I tried to release the contact, the man took my hand more firmly, indicating that I was to stay. At that moment I became aware that a hidden vitality was passing between us. I do not know if he was giving something to me, or asking something of me, but I understood that at some level of being those silent moments mattered.

What is it that makes many of us so anxious about drawing close to a person in pain? May it not be that we are afraid? If that is the case, what are the grounds of such fear? The following story from the Talmud may help to throw some light on this question. It concerns a bedside visit made by no less a person than the great Rabbi Yochanan. Rabbi Yochanan, who lived and taught during the third century of our era in the land of Israel, was famed for his great beauty as well as his wisdom, as the story bears out. He was clearly well accomplished at the pastoral task, for we are told that on a previous visit he managed not only to comfort but even to cure the patient. Subsequently, however, he had himself fallen ill, but was fortunate enough to receive similar help from a colleague. Typically, the Talmud wants to know why, if he was so successful a healer, he couldn't cure himself. The text notes wryly in answer that 'no man can free himself from prison'. In other words, we are all dependent, from the least to the greatest, on one another. This, perhaps, is the message of the more complex scene which follows:

Rabbi Elazar fell ill and Rabbi Yochanan went in to visit him. He found him lying in a dark chamber. He bared his arm and the room filled with light. He noticed that Rabbi Elazar was weeping. He said to him:
'Why are you weeping? If it is because of the Torah you

haven't yet learned, have we not said: it is all the same whether one does little or whether one does much, so long as the heart is directed towards Heaven?'

(Evidently there was no answer, so Rabbi Yochanan continued:)

'If it's because of your poverty [that you are weeping], not everyone is fortunate enough to have two tables (both wealth and Torah).'

(When Rabbi Elazar again did not answer, he asked a third time:)

'If it is on account of children that you are weeping (that is, because Rabbi Elazar either had no children or had lost them,) then this is the bone of my tenth son.'

Rabbi Elazar said to him: 'It is because beauty such as yours must wither in the dust that I weep.'

'That,' said Rabbi Yochanan, 'is worth weeping for', and he too wept.[9]

What is the point of this half humorous and half sad story? It surely has more to tell us than the simple message that it is important to visit the sick. The purpose lies rather in the response of Rabbi Elazar to Rabbi Yochanan's questions and in the fact that both men subsequently weep. Rabbi Yochanan looks at the patient, notices the tears, but then proceeds to make assumptions of his own. There must be something wrong in Rabbi Elazar's life; why else would he be crying? He hasn't studied enough Torah; he hasn't enough money; it's something to do with children. Aren't these the reasons why people weep? But in each case a silent response proves these suggestions to be wide of the mark. Eventually an answer comes from Rabbi Elazar which touches right on Rabbi Yochanan's most vulnerable spot: You came in here so sure of your own gifts, you bared your arm and filled the room with light, you confidently reconciled me with my fate. What you have omitted to consider is that you too are mortal and that even beauty such as yours

86

must wither in the dust. Recognizing the truth of the statement, Rabbi Yochanan too begins to weep. It is at this moment that he becomes a true companion. Until then he has been filled with judgments and assumptions of his own; from now on he is truly there with and for his younger colleague. The story ends, like the previous incidents, on a happy note: Rabbi Yochanan reaches out his hand and raises Rabbi Elazar up from his sickbed. But the point this time is that he remains unable to help until the moment when he realizes that he too is vulnerable and will perish in the dust. Why, one might ask, didn't he feel this before? Who can tell? Maybe the story gives us a clue in the reference to the death of Rabbi Yochanan's ten sons. Perhaps he had simply experienced too much suffering already to want to have that pain opened up once more. Or maybe he was the kind of person who gave so much of himself and spent so much time among the sick that it had all become something of a routine – till his true sensibilities were awakened once again.

For whatever reasons, be they temporary, due to the particular pressures that weigh on us at the moment, or more permanent, most of us strive to protect ourselves against the painful invasion of the experience of our own vulnerability. But until we do face our own mortality, until we can sit quietly and not entirely defended next to our fellow human being in pain, there will be things which we will choose not to know and from which we will have to avert our gaze. That is not to say that we should take on other people's suffering as if it were our own. Other people's pain is not our pain, and we have to consider what it means to them, not what it means to us. Noisy professions of empathy may sometimes amount to little more than self indulgence. On the contrary, being there means withdrawing to let the other be. But we have to be prepared to listen to all that may be said. We need to stop ourselves preventing it from being said, albeit unconsciously, by implication, by tacit signs that we do not want to hear, even if it is about loneliness, or sickness, or the fate of one's children after one's death.

The Torah, as noted earlier, insists that we may not 'hide ourselves away' from the suffering of someone else's animal, let alone from that of a fellow human being. This is Isaiah's message in a famous passage which we read on the morning of the Day of Atonement:

Is not this the fast that I have chosen ...
Is it not to deal thy bread to the hungry,
And that thou bring the poor that are cast out to thy house?
When thou seest the naked, that thou cover him,
And that thou hide not thyself from thine own flesh

(Isa. 58.6–7).

In the last line Isaiah employs the very same verb the Torah had used earlier in reference to our responsibility towards the stray or overburdened animal. The two passages share a common principle: that we may not hide ourselves away, that we are not free to pretend we didn't notice. But, whether he meant it or not, the prophet's words go further in suggesting a deeper reason why we often do not want to know. Careful reading suggests that the root of all the actions he describes is the last; unless we are prepared to face our own flesh, we will find it hard to meet any of the other demands of which the prophet speaks. What then does that final phrase mean? It can be understood both literally and metaphorically. In the latter sense it teaches us that the flesh, the nakedness and need, of our fellow beings should be to us as our own. In the former it instructs us specifically to be aware of our own flesh, our own mortality, our own susceptibility to all those things to which, by virtue of being human, we are inevitably exposed. Then, the prophet's words imply, if we are brave enough to face our own frailty we will also find the courage to confront and care about the needs of others. Just as the person who has been an exile is most intimately acquainted with the needs of the stranger, so the one who can acknowledge that he too will die is best able to listen to the fears of the dying. Facing our own flesh we know that there is nothing else we have to hide from. Out of that very smallness we draw courage and learn to appreciate both the privileges and the responsibilities of being human.

6. *Do not separate yourself from the community (Hillel, in Chapters of the Fathers 2.5)*

Only in the group, only in society as a whole, can the values which stem from the principle of *gemilut hesed* be fully expressed.

Although nothing can replace the individual and though, as we have seen, trust and generosity ultimately depend on the quality of the relationship of one individual with another, and even of that individual with him- or herself, the context of *gemilut hesed* is really the group. It is not a matter which starts and stops at home, to be confined to the privacy of the one-to-one relationship; it must be articulated in and through the ethos of the entire community. Life in the stetls and towns of Eastern Europe provides an excellent example of what can be achieved. When one studies the social history of those communities, one is frequently impressed by the range of institutions they created to provide for each other's needs. Ideally, there would be the Chevrat Bikkur Cholim to take responsibility for visiting the sick and the Chevra Kaddisha to ensure that every person, rich or poor, was buried with dignity. There was the fund for the itinerant poor whose needs were as basic as food for the rest of the day, and the fund for the resident poor whose needs were to be provided for from week to week. There was the Hachnasat Kallah dowry fund to ensure that the poor or fatherless bride could enter the married state with pride. There was, as if one had to mention it, the scholarship fund to enable all children to have an elementary education, and a range of communal strategies to support the advanced but indigent student of Torah. It was understood that should that most urgent of all demands arise, the need to ransom hostages – whose very lives

would otherwise be in danger – then, as the Talmud and following it Maimonides had ruled, money could be diverted from
any of the above causes for that purpose.[10] There was nothing
'artificial' or consciously 'benevolent' about any of these institutions, though doubtless they often had their faults. They
simply were, and since time immemorial always had been, an
essential part of what a community did. They were a basic and
practical expression of its values, the realization of the words of
the Talmud recited every morning:

> These are the things, the fruits of which a person enjoys in
> this world, while the stock remains in the world to come:
> Honouring one's father and mother, acts of faithful love,
> early attendance at the house of study morning and evening,
> hospitality to guests, visiting the sick, providing for a bride,
> escorting the dead, devotion in prayer and making peace
> between a person and their fellow; and the study of Torah
> leads to them all.[11]

These traditions help to explain why so many Jewish people
are so committed to the health and helping professions. Indeed,
it has been noted that a number of key institutions of the
welfare state were developed from an observation of the way
the Jewish community treated the sick and provided for the
needy. Thus there is a certain continuity between the Jewish
past and some of the caring establishments of today's societies.
However, there are also differences. The most important of
these is that in the stetl welfare issues were regarded as the
immediate concern of the individual and the local community.
There were no large, anonymous and invisible bodies to whom
such matters were delegated. Responsibility thus remained with
each community rather than with the state, and every person
who formed part of that community was directly answerable for
the values it expressed and the actions it undertook. In recent
times there have been attempts to return to such a model, the
much-quoted slogan of the British government 'care in the

community' being an obvious example. But unfortunately many of the prerequisites are lacking. Most significantly, the feeling of community has itself been eroded. At present there does not appear to exist, at least in most of the Western world, the sense of mutual responsibility, of shared values and of collective identity that would allow it to re-emerge.

The lack of community in modern society serves only to enhance the value of what Judaism has always taught, and to help us to understand the emphasis it places on the responsibility to be part of the group. To pursue an isolated course is certainly possible; to live an isolated but full Jewish life is not. There are duties which cannot be performed unless one is part of a larger unit. Though these belong specifically to the domain of prayer – one cannot recite the Kaddish, hear the repetition of the Amidah or read the Torah except in a *minyan* (a quorum of at least ten)[12] – the effect is felt across the whole extent of Jewish life. It could even be argued that the penalization of the isolated individual by means of the sanction of religious disadvantages was a conscious and deliberate way of applying pressure to make him or her join the congregation, a step which was perceived as essential for much broader reasons. An examination of the origins of the concept of the *minyan* might bear this out. Two derivations are commonly given for why the *minyan*, the minimum number needed to form a quorum, consists of ten. According to the first, this number is learnt, albeit indirectly, by following a series of verbal links, from the ten spies who undermined the morale of the people of Israel as it stood poised to enter the promised land. According to the second, the origin of the number is to be sought in Abraham's argument with God regarding the fate of Sodom, in which the smallest group of righteous people for whose sake he begs God to avert the destruction of the city is likewise ten. What the two groups of ten have in common is that in each case they are perceived as the minimum unit capable of influencing the fate of a much larger population. The *minyan* may thus be defined as the smallest socially effective group. Ten represents the lowest number of people among whom values can so be expressed as to have an impact on an entire society. Ten have serious moral influence. Nehama Leibowitz gives this idea its full weight in her analysis of why in his bargaining with God over the fate of Sodom Abraham refers specifically to the need for a certain minimum number of righteous persons *within* the city. Why does Abraham particularly stress the fact that these people have to be *within*, rather than just in, Sodom?

> The few can turn the scales and save the place, if the righteous individuals concerned are 'within the city', playing a promi-nent part in public life and exerting their influence in its many fields of activity. But if they merely exist, living in retirement and never venturing forth but pursuing their pious conduct unseen and unknown, they will, perhaps, save themselves, but will certainly not possess the spiritual merit capable of pro-tecting the city. The same city which forces the righteous few into retirement so that their scrupulous moral standards should not interfere with the injustice dominating public life, that same city is not entitled to claim salvation by virtue of the handful of righteous men leading a secluded life within it.[13]

However much, then, the individual is the source of moral good, it is the group, the community, which allows that good to be effectively expressed. *Gemilut hesed* can therefore be given its fullest potential only within the context of a society which strives towards and affirms those values which the principle would otherwise represent in theory alone. But there is also another, a more insidious and disturbing reason, for seeking to be part of a society which has sound and beneficent values. 'Till the very day of death,' teaches Hillel in the same passage from which the title to this section is taken 'do not rely on yourself.' His purpose in saying this was not to undermine our confidence in the value of the individual but rather to remind us of our frailty. Who can know what temptations and pressures he or she will be exposed to, and how he or she will react to them when the real test comes? This is brought home by a remarkable interpretation of an apparently insignificant detail in the story of the spies referred to above. The Talmud notes that whereas all twelve emissaries set out together, only one of them chose to travel via Hebron. This, a typical example of its exegetical acumen, is learned by the Talmud from an otherwise inexplicable change from plural to singular of the verb which describes the group's travels: 'They went up (plural) through the Negev and came (singular) to Hebron' (Num.13.22).[14] But which of the spies was it who visited Hebron? It was Caleb. What did he have to do there, and why did he go on his own? He went because that is where the matriarchs and patriarchs were buried, and he wanted to prostrate himself on their graves and pray for the strength to withstand the pressures which he already knew the other spies would exert on him during the journey and when they returned to the camp. The message our rabbis wished to convey is clear: only a fool takes for granted his ability to go it alone. Every child knows the power of peer pressure, and the lesson is brought home at every stage of life: however strong one's resolve may be, it is hard to resist the bullying demands of the majority. It is better to avoid temptation. It was the old mistake of Lot to think that he could go to Sodom and live a good life in a vicious environment. Whoever imagines likewise merely repeats the error. We should be profoundly grateful for the protection a decent society gives us, not just from others but from ourselves. We should be thankful if we are not forced to discover all that we may be capable of. Judaism takes a realistic view of human nature; we are not born evil, but neither are we immune to its influence. It would be a rash person who was confident that there were certain things 'I could never ever bring myself to do.'

I shall not forget an encounter I had two years ago with a lady in her early fifties. It happened in the church hall of a small town in southern Germany. I had just finished answering the audience's questions about a talk I had given on the subject of Judaism today, when the woman came up to me and asked if we could have a few words alone together.

'You are the first Jewish person I've met for almost fifty years,' she said. 'The last time I saw one was during the war. Late at night there was a sudden, desperate knocking on the door. Hesitantly, my father opened it. Outside stood a young Jew with a beard. He was thin and very hungry. "Give me some bread," he begged. My father slammed the door.'

The woman turned away to weep.

'In all these years my mother and I have never been able to forget that face. It haunts me all the time.'

I felt, not for the first time in Germany, what a terrible thing it must have been to have belonged to a society which legitimated and nourished evil. How impossible, how terrible are the situations to which its citizens are exposed! How difficult it must be, what courage it must take, to resist! I am deeply grateful not to have had to live in a country which legalizes the bestial and persecutes the good. Nazi Germany is, thank God, no more. But there are many evil places, and there is much bad and even more indifference within most societies.

The price of freedom, it has rightly been said, is eternal vigilance. Only the naive can imagine that prejudice, hatred and despotism will simply go away. The duty to fight against them devolves upon everyone. The enemy is not only malice but the cosy neglect in which the sentinels of freedom sing themselves to sleep. We must never allow the law, the press or any of those many organs which together form the ethos of a culture, to be instruments of wrong. A society that is good facilitates greater good. A society that is bad, complacent, cruel or corrupt, soon fosters those conditions where evil breeds, even in hearts that did not know they could be hosts to things so vile.

7. *Who my neighbour is*

However important it may be to live as part of the community, community itself is not the panacea for all ills. The danger, especially of a religious group, is that its concerns may extend no further than itself. However universal the overt message, the unspoken reality is liable to be as follows: 'If you're in, if you're one of us, we'll do everything for you. If you're out, if you're not one of us, we'll do very little.' At worst, religions have not only rejected but demonized the 'other', those who don't belong, turning them into implacable enemies and attributing to them all ills. The explanations for this lie partly in the fear most people and especially most groups have for those they do not know, partly in the attitude that 'there is but one truth and we have it' and partly in the need to live in an unambiguous world where all good is within and all bad without. For these reasons I agree with the person who once said that the real measure of the morality of a community is how it behaves towards those who are not part of it. The subject to which I therefore turn is the question of our responsibility towards other groups and for wrongs inflicted on anyone, whether or not they affect us directly.

A telling indication in this regard is how we understand the brief but central commandment 'Thou shalt love thy neighbour as thyself, I am the Lord' (Lev. 19.18). Who, after all, is our neighbour? Is our neighbour only the person who literally lives next door, or is our neighbour all humankind? It has rightly been said that the idea that one can love humanity as a whole is absurd; such love is the province of the idealist and usually amounts to very little. On the other hand, too many people are guilty of the opposite extreme. Unconsciously, perhaps, they place a different emphasis on the famous commandment, construing it to mean 'Thou shalt love thy neighbour who is like thyself.' So long as they're 'one of us' all well and good; however, let them be different in race, religion, nationality, or even habits, and we are exempted from the obligation to care about them at all. Let them go to the devil! Perhaps, indeed, they actually are the devil.

Every day brings some new outrage. As I write, my mind is full of the pictures of men shovelling snow in Sarajevo: red snow, from the blood of six children whose sin was no more than to seek a few hours of joy amidst the difficulties of their lives. They were playing on their toboggans when two shells fell in their midst. I have never before seen the leader of a people struggle not to cry, but the Bosnian Prime Minister was trying very hard not to weep when he said in a television interview that the blame for this despicable act was to be laid firstly at the gates of those who had fired the weapons, but secondly at the doors of all the indifferent nations who allowed such things to be. These children don't live next door like the families in my street, but are they not my neighbours as described in that demanding sentence: 'Don't stand idly by your neighbour's blood' (Lev. 19.16)? What, then, am I to do?

There is a great temptation to say 'This is not my issue', to ask the questions 'Are they Jewish? or Christian? or white? or black?', and, when the response comes in the negative, to breath a sigh of relief and depart exonerated from the arena of moral duty. But this is not good enough. It shows a selfish morality, and it is ultimately no good for the self. When something is a human issue it is my issue. Deeper than my definition of my self as a member of my family is my definition of myself as a member of my people; deeper than my definition of myself as a member of my people is my definition of myself as a human being. It is a truism that I hurt in the same way as you hurt, that, as Shakespeare made Shylock say, I bleed in the same way as you bleed. Martin Luther King, surely one of the great moral leaders of the twentieth century, wrote a letter during his imprisonment in Birmingham City Jail which has justly become famous. In it he addressed those who saw his wider activities in the civil rights movement as 'unwise and untimely'. What, they asked, had he been doing so far from his own home? Why had he felt it necessary to get involved in the concerns of some distant locality? In his response Martin Luther King wrote that like the prophets of the Old Testament and the apostles of the New, he felt obliged to leave his home town and take his message of justice to where it was needed: 'I am cognizant of the interrelatedness of all communities and states. I cannot sit idly by in Atlanta and not be concerned about what happens in Birmingham. Injustice anywhere is a threat to justice everywhere. We are caught in an inescapable network of mutuality, tied in a single garment of destiny.'[15] When evil is done, we may not say 'it is not my issue'; it is.

What, then, are we to do about it? Our obligations can be defined in terms of three imperatives: we must not make ourselves wilfully ignorant, we must not be silent and we must not abandon the hope that action is worthwhile. Whereas they may be expressed as negatives, these three demands constitute a call for active, constant and immediate moral commitment.

Cain's response has been considered earlier. Perhaps, however, there are occasions when it is better to say 'I do not know'? Perhaps we should not burden the heart with the pain of millions for whom we can do nothing? Certainly it is the case that we are overloaded with images of suffering: watching starving children on our television screens, or the slaughter of civilians in some despicable act of savagery, has been described as one of the original rituals of the late twentieth century. Such pictures soon cease to have the impact they should. Certainly there is no point in indulging in them for the sake of it. But to remain completely ignorant is totally unjustifiable. To refuse to see beyond the walls of one's own home or to care about anything beyond the confines of one's immediate community is not good enough. Such 'silent pockets of goodness' are often precisely what permit injustices to spread all around – and eventually to engulf – them, just because they are no more than silent pockets. Ignorance of others is, furthermore, often the beginning of the fear of others, and fear of others is the cause, in part at least, of prejudices about them. It is easier to regard as less than human that kind or colour of person into whose home one has never been, with whom one has never conversed or formed acquaintance. 'I don't know' is only too frequently the prelude to 'I don't care'. Loving one's neighbour as oneself must therefore include asking oneself awkward questions about who our neighbours are and having the courage to extend the boundaries of our moral commitments even in ways which challenge our assumptions and threaten our insularity.

When we know, we are duty bound not to remain silent. 'How can there be anything wrong with silence?' one may ask. The answer is that silence empowers. But unlike moral courage, which empowers those who dare to speak out, silence empowers the perpetrators of crime. Passivity, whatever inner attitude it may in fact conceal, amounts in practice to implied assent. Afterwards we may say, 'I was never party to this', or 'I never agreed to what those brutes were doing', but one can say it afterwards till the cows come home. At the time we said nothing; we lacked the courage or the commitment or the conviction. We were bystanders, that's all. We played our silent part.

We have a moral duty to dissociate ourselves from evil. Furthermore, we have to do so quickly, for in such matters time is usually only on one's side for a limited period. Thereafter it becomes increasingly difficult to speak out. Soon evil has such a hold upon society that well-founded fear cripples all but the very bravest. The list of ills which society did indeed have power to stop – once – is virtually endless. Pastor Niemöller's words are justifiably famous, but there are few signs that his message has been heard:

First they came for the Jews
and I did not speak out because I was not a Jew.

Then they came for the communists
and I did not speak out because I was not a communist.

Then they came for the trade unionists
and I did not speak out because I was not a trade unionist.

Then they came for me
and there was no one left to speak out for me.

One asks oneself the question: 'If I speak out, what difference
will it make anyway?' The answer is that the difference may be
greater than one can possibly know. During the entire period of
his imprisonment in the Lebanon, the envoy of the Archbishop
of Canterbury, Terry Waite, was doubtless sent thousands, tens
of thousands, of letters. Only one got through; but that one
letter made a very great difference to him. Proof of this is the
fact that it was among the very first things he spoke about on
his release. One has to imagine that what one is doing, the
letter you and I are writing, is the only letter which will get
through. What if the person who wrote that card to Terry Waite
had said, 'It will never reach him', and had given up?

But it was not only that one letter which mattered; the effect
of all the letters which never arrived was also very great. Each
one of them carried the message to the censors who destroyed it
that the writer could not condone behaviour of such a kind. 'So
what?', one might ask. But the power of dissent should not
be underestimated. Feeble as it may frequently seem, dissent
punctures by the very fact of its existence the confidence of the
perpetrators of evil. They are not so much in control as they had
thought. Here is a voice that cannot be silenced, a freedom that
cannot be removed. Every message to the powerful that power
is not truth proves its point: ultimately nothing can destroy the
liberty of the human voice and the human mind. However much
they may persecute others, oppressors are persecuted in turn
by the inevitability of their failure. Perhaps it is the very knowledge that he cannot and will not succeed that makes the
tyrant so cruel. Exiled under Stalin to Voronezh, the poet
Osip Mandelstam gives courageous expression to the ultimate
impotence of power in its battle against freedom and truth:

You took away all the oceans and all the room.
You gave me my shoe-size in earth with bars around it.
Where did it get you? Nowhere.
You left me my lips, and they shape words, even in silence.[16]

Be this as it may, it is all too easy to lose heart. To preserve a sense of the value of one's actions and the meaning of human life, even in the midst of the utmost difficulties, requires not only great courage but also much wisdom. This point is made most forcefully, but also most gently, in a short sermon about one of the most bitter experiences in Jewish history:

It happened once when the Emperor Hadrian was passing through on his way to wage war and was marching with his legions to fight against a certain country which had rebelled against him, that he came upon an old man who was planting young fig trees. Hadrian said to him:
'Old man, here you are putting in all this effort and going to all this trouble for the sake of others!'
The old man replied to Hadrian:
'My master the king! I am planting trees. Should I be found worthy, I shall eat of the fruits of my planting. If not, my children will eat of them.'
Hadrian waged war for three years. At the end of this time he returned. What did the old man do? He took a bowl and filled it with the first fruits of beautiful figs and brought them before Hadrian. He said to him:
'My master the king! I am the same old man whom you came across when you first set out. You said to me then: "Old man, here you are going to all this trouble and bother for the sake of others." But look, the Holy, Blessed One, has already granted me to eat of the fruits of my planting, and here they are in this bowl.'
Then Hadrian said to his servant: 'Take the bowl from him and fill it with gold coins.'[17]

Hadrian was the Roman emperor, the most powerful person in the world. The country against whom he was waging war was presumably none other than Judaea, which had rebelled against him under the leadership of Bar Kochba. During the bitter and bloody campaign hundreds of thousands, millions according to some sources, were killed, and the country was laid waste. Is that a time when anyone would think of planting? Yet one old man, considering not himself but the needs of the future and the good of the world as a whole, keeping faith with life and land, went ahead and planted. In so doing he achieved more than the Emperor himself in all his three years of war. For what did Hadrian have to show for his long and bloody efforts? – Hills and valleys full of corpses and a countryside laid waste. But the old man had a bowl of figs to show for his three years, and a tree, the tree of life his own meagre hands had planted.

There are many ways to express moral resistance and solidarity with humanity, our neighbour. Many kinds of conduct may be faithful.

8. 'Whither I go ...'

'The human being is always considered forewarned, whether his action be inadvertent or deliberate, whether he be asleep or awake,' rules the Mishnah.[18] The statement appears in the context of the laws of damages, where a differentiation is made with regard to the extent of liability depending on the degree to which the cause or causer of harm can be held responsible for what has been done. But it requires little imagination to extend the application of the Mishnah to life as a whole. The human being is answerable for what he or she does in absolutely every case. The action may have been inadvertent; we may not have been aware of the probable results, we may have acted in misguided innocence, there may have been extenuating circumstances. But none of these explanations constitutes an excuse sufficient to exculpate us entirely from any responsibility for the consequences of our actions. Whether on our own or in a greater unit, as part of our particular group or in the context of society as a whole, we are answerable for what we do. There is no escape from the burden of responsibility. There is no time and no place when we are permitted to desist from acting according to what we perceive to be right and true. There is no situation of which we can say that it absolutely doesn't matter what we do.

This truth has been presented not just from a humanist but from a specifically religious perspective. We have defined *gemilut hesed* as such conduct as befits and fosters the relationship of faith which links God and humankind together in mutual responsibility. Our moral and our spiritual selves are thus bound to one another. One cannot rightly seek to be close to God while distancing oneself from the needs of other people. Conversely, without spiritual commitment and inspiration we deprive ourselves not only of a significant portion of our moral vision, but also of some of the most precious resources available to us with which to try to meet the everyday challenge of being a compassionate and responsive human being. God inspires us, yet exacts from us; awaits our response, yet pursues us to the depths of our conscience, searching our kidneys and our heart. Our relationship with God is coextensive with our relationship with life; nowhere does the bond of *hesed* release us from its demands:

Whither shall I go from Thy spirit?
Or whither shall I flee from Thy Presence?
If I ascend up into heaven, Thou art there;
If I make my bed in the nether world, behold, Thou art there.
If I take the wings of the morning,
And dwell in the uttermost parts of the sea;
Even there would Thy hand lead me,
And Thy right would hold me.
And if I say: 'Surely the darkness shall envelop me,

And the light about me shall be night';
Even the darkness is not too dark for Thee,
But the night shineth as the day;
The darkness is even as the light (Psalm 139.7–12).

There can be no such a thing as hiding oneself away, either morally nor spiritually. Distant as their effects may be, our actions point back at us as the circumference of the circle indicates the centre. How much it matters, then, how we act! How crucial, above all, is our attitude within ourselves, the degree to which our mind and heart are open, faithful, aware of the vulnerable privileges of being mortal, being flesh.

IV

The Hidden God

And while You are uplifted over them
Upon a throne exalted and high
Yet are You more near to them
Than their own bodies, their own souls

(Yehudah Halevi)

1. *A question of language*

Once, when I was too little to remember, we went for a family holiday to Pitlochry in the central highlands of Scotland and stayed in a small hotel. The institution must have been some-what out of the ordinary because my older brother is reputed to have said that its porter was none other than God. Upon further questioning he explained that just like God, the porter seemed to know everything, see everything, do everything and most certainly carry everything. The story is revealing, not only about my brother's perspicacity and early religious zeal, but also about the way in which we talk to young children, and indeed to everybody else, about God. God is omnipresent; there is no place from which He is absent for so long as a fraction of one second. God is omniscient; He sees not only round corners but, rather more disturbingly, through the skin and flesh as far as the very heart, and through the past and present into the unrevealed future. God is omnipotent; everything is within His capacity and if, in a given instance, He refrains from acting, it is assuredly out of choice and not for lack of the ability to do so. God is all-wise, all-good and all-forgiving; if anything bad happens it must be our fault not God's, and in the long run anyway God means it all for the best. God, in short, is totally beyond any of the limitations that impinge upon the human being; everybody else is dependent and must constantly be reminded of that fact, but God is of course sufficient unto Himself.

This image of God is reinforced by much of the language of the prayer book which speaks to us of the Lord who is 'great, mighty and terrible', 'who revives the dead with great mercy, sustains the falling, heals the sick and frees the bound', who 'knows our thoughts' and who 'tests the heart'. It is, of course, to be understood that none of these phrases is necessarily to be taken in the sense in which we would understand it were it referring to another human being; all language falls short of portraying the almighty and unknowable God. But the descriptions nevertheless leave the intended impression of a being who is beyond all limitation, awesome in power and infinite in capacity. They often leave a sense of fear and remoteness as well.

What doesn't necessarily reinforce this image of God is our experience of the world. The moment that is taken into account the matter becomes more difficult. Most of the words used to describe God either take us beyond our experience or appear to run counter to it. The classic questions are familiar: if God is everywhere, why is God not here now, and if God is here now and God is also all good, then why doesn't God do something about the state of the world? The issues which provoke those challenges are on the one hand infinitely varied; they move from the individual sickbed to the vale of Babi Yar, where the Jewish population of Kiev was slaughtered by the Nazis. On the other hand they are always the same: the injustice of unmerited suffering in the – supposed – presence of a God who is benign. In the face of such a critique theology has generally sought refuge in the truism that the Lord is beyond our understanding: 'For My thoughts are not your thoughts, nor are your ways My ways, says the Lord. For as the heavens are higher than the earth, so are My ways higher than your ways and My thoughts than your thoughts' (Isa. 55.8,9). We can do no more than confess our ignorance of the secrets of God's exalted plans, and accept our fate with dignity and trust. In times of trouble the suffering individual must be counselled to seek solace in the hope that, as the Talmud puts it, God inclines towards mercy and that maybe prayer and good deeds will persuade Him to avert the evil decree.[1]

But it is not only to those who reject the idea of His existence that the way we usually speak about God makes no sense; it also fails to do justice to the intuitions of many of those who seek, and the confirmed experiences of many of those who actively pursue, their faith. This is not because one comes to feel that God is less than all present or other than all good, but rather because the distance implied by such absolute and incomprehensible terms fails to articulate the sense of a close, immediate and mutual relationship. One is drawn, therefore, to search for words with greater power to express what the heart has known. Ultimately, of course, the venture is bound to failure; before the realization of God's greatness language fades into abstractions, into silence. Nevertheless, for the sake of our own human need, and to find companions on this journey of the spirit, one seeks a mode of expression more vivid, more able to articulate the feelings of heart and soul.

Perhaps it is true of many religions that it is the mystics above all who, turning to God the infinite, address that unknowable presence as God the parent, God the partner, and especially as God the lover or the beloved. The prototype for such language is, of course, the Bible itself, which is permeated with such personal, intimate imagery. Indeed, it is so full of terms which ascribe not only human feelings but even human form – hands, fingers and eyes – to God, that part of the long Jewish tradition of translation and exegesis can be seen as a 'clean-up job' to remove the stumbling block of anthropomorphic misconceptions from before the naive reader. But to devote oneself mercilessly to such a task is to miss the fact that we have a need for these personal expressions. The very frequency with which they occur testifies to the fact that we relate to God on the emotional level as much as, if not more than, on the intellectual. They enable us to combine the rigorous, but abstract, pursuit of ideas with the living of an immediate relationship. For God is apprehended as the direct object of feeling rather than as the distant object of thought. Furthermore, God, as we shall presently consider, is said to share some of the very same feelings that we feel.

To what, though, do such expressions as 'God the parent' or 'God the lover' amount? They are perhaps no more, it might be claimed, than the extension of anthropomorphism to anthropopathism, the use of terms drawn from human experience to describe not only who God is, but how God feels and how we feel towards God. But just as God in the former case has neither hands nor eyes nor mouth, so in the latter God feels neither affection nor pain in the way that we do: it is all only metaphor, a vain attempt to portray the unknowable. True as this must ultimately be, the language of relationship and emotion does articulate one important difference in the way in which God is perceived, a change indicative of more than words alone. It portrays God not as above, beyond and independent of humanity, but rather as close to and in relationship with, indeed even at times dependent upon, us. God, in Heschel's famous phrase, is in search of the human being as much as the human being is in search of God. This mutuality is an inevitable, indeed an intended and desired, consequence of creation. For in fashioning us as free agents God linked the divine fate and fortune with our own. From the moment God said 'let us make man in our image', choosing to form a partner rather than a pawn, God became bound to a relationship with us, entrusting us with the divine name and reputation, rendering Himself susceptible to hurt at our hands. God could of course destroy the world and end the partnership, but Jewish tradition perceives Him as choosing out of mercy not to do so, in order to work with us, despite our faults, towards redemption.

In this concluding chapter, some of the implications of thinking about God from such a perspective, as interdependent with and even in some sense dependent on human beings, will be explored. As in the rest of this book, material has been drawn both from traditional rabbinic sources and from conversations and encounters with people. It is presented in the hope that such a way of speaking about God may be helpful to those who, like the writer, care deeply about the religious quest, but find in absolutes and abstractions an inadequate tool for exploring and explaining either the intimation of God's presence or the painful challenge of the apparent Divine absence or for addressing the unanswerable questions of how we and God interrelate.

2. God's vulnerability

Rarely has the importance of how we think and talk about God been brought home to me more immediately than at a seminar I recently attended in a local hospice on the subject of 'If there is a God, then why does He or She let this happen to me?'. Among the speakers was a member from the Humanist Society who had been invited to address the gathering from the point of view of an agnostic. This was particularly relevant, because many of the patients at the hospice profess to be of no formal religion or to have no faith other than in name alone. The man spoke eloquently about the way in which death gives meaning to each moment of our lives. Without death life would not be precious. We would not value it, appreciate its beauty or feel sufficiently motivated to develop a sense of purpose during our brief existence. This, he said, was how he would counsel a sick person who came to the Society for support in mortal illness or console a family member or friend suffering the pain of bereavement. Death helps to give meaning and urgency to life. People, he observed, appreciate this message.

He then turned to the question of why so many come to the

Humanist Society for comfort, rather than go to the representatives of the faiths of their ancestors. Many, he noted, choose to do so out of disenchantment with a religion which they are sure will offer them no solace. For religions, people believe, point the finger at the sufferer. God the perfect, the all-knowing, they assume they will be told, is punishing you for your misdeeds. Why else, after all, if there is a God, would that God want someone to be ill? According to religion, suffering is the just, if bitter, fruit of doing wrong. The understandable unwillingness to accept such a view, preached openly by some ministers and tacitly implied by others, drives many people to the Humanist Society and persuades them to adopt an agnostic or atheist attitude.

In the discussion which followed, a number of members of the clergy present challenged the suppositions on which this argument was based. They responded to the speaker by saying that they did not perceive God in such a punitive manner at all. Interpretations of suffering and misery as the expression of God's judgment and condemnation were, it was felt, misrepresentations of what religion had to say about such matters. Certainly they did not encompass the whole truth. Surely there were other ways of thinking about God in the kind of tragic situations we were speaking about. 'When I'm with someone ill,' one minister eventually said, 'I see God as suffering too'. As I listened to this discussion, there came into my mind the rabbinic teaching that one who visits the ill is forbidden to sit higher than the patient because 'the Divine Presence rests above the pillow of the sick'.[2] In one way this is of course a truism: God is everywhere. But the point of the saying is that here the Lord is manifestly present; the sickbed matters especially to God. We are asked to remember that this is the God of whom Isaiah said: 'In all their affliction He was afflicted' (63.9). How then could God be absent from a hospital bed? There is, furthermore, a second and no less significant purpose to the saying: it is not as the accuser apportioning blame, not as the one who afflicts, that we are taught to think of God, but rather as the one who comforts and consoles, as the one who suffers too.

This idea has a long and important history in Jewish thought. It begins, as just noted, with the Bible and it continues till the last days of the Warsaw Ghetto and up to the present time. Although there are many sources in the Bible from which the understanding that God suffers with His creatures can be derived, in later literature one or other of two key verses is generally quoted. The first is that from Isaiah referred to above, the second the simple statement of the Psalmist: 'I am with [each person] in trouble' (Psalm 91.15). Since in Jewish history and thought the epitome of all suffering is exile, we may add to the above verses Deuteronomy 30.3: 'The Lord will come back with your captivity', which suggests that God not only feels our pain but also shares our homeless condition. For one would have expected, as Rashi, following rabbinic precedent, points out, that the sentence would read 'The Lord will bring back your captivity'. But the use of the simple rather than the causative form of the verb, 'come back with' instead of 'bring back', teaches us that God's presence has gone into exile with us and will stay there with us until it and we return together. These two insights, that God suffers our anguish alongside us and descends with us into captivity, are put together in a classic answer to the question why God chose to reveal Himself to Moses in a thorn-bush rather than in any other type of plant:

> Apply [to this situation] the text (Song of Songs 5.2): 'Open to me, my dove, my twin.' Just as with twins, if one has a headache, the other also feels it, so it is with the Holy, blessed One (Psalm 91.15): 'I will be with him in trouble.' Said the Holy, blessed One, to Moses: Don't you feel that I suffer anguish whenever Israel does? Know, therefore, from the character of the place from which I am speaking to you, out of the thornbush, that I, as it were, share their suffering.[3]

But if God suffers, in what way does God suffer? In a remarkable passage, the Talmud tells of how Rabbi Yossei, a sage who lived in the second century of our era, entered one of the many ruined buildings of Jerusalem, destroyed when the Romans captured the city and burnt down the Temple. Although, as the Talmud notes, he should rather have avoided such a place for reasons of both safety and reputation, he chooses to go in and meditate there. There is evidently a symbolic dimension to his conduct: Rabbi Yossei is all too aware of the tragic fate and constant sufferings of his people, epitomized by the devastation of Jerusalem. Pondering these matters, entering the ruins in his thought, he asks himself not only what these things mean on a human level but also what they signify for God. When he emerges from his contemplations Elijah the Prophet is there to meet him. He asks the rabbi what he has heard inside the ruined building: 'A voice moaning like a dove,' he answers, 'and saying "alas for the children on account of whose sins I have destroyed My house and exiled them among the nations".' When he learns that Rabbi Yossei has had such an experience Elijah at once enlarges upon it, telling him that every day when Israel praise Him, God nods His head and says 'Happy is the King whom they praise thus in His house; alack for the father who has exiled his children and alas for the children, banished from their father's table.'[4] We see here a God who is lonely, who mourns for the absent children, who longs for their company and sorrows over their fate (a fate which, it must be noted, He Himself had felt obliged to apportion). The story speaks of a God who pays the price of partnership. The implication is that far from being some abrupt and arbitrary deity who feels no bonds of friendship, God cannot even sever them when the case demands. Deeper than justice is love. God suffers for being a parent and is, like the human counterpart, afflicted by His children's sorrow. It is surely no accident that the voice heard by Rabbi Yossei has the sound of a dove. It was believed that out of all the birds the dove alone formed no second bond at the loss of its mate, but mourned patiently, awaiting the return of its partner. God, too, like the faithful bird, sorrows and waits.

In a no less famous passage God is described as suffering without speech. What is the meaning, asks the Talmud, of Jeremiah's words (13.17) 'in secret places does my soul weep'? 'Rav Shmuel bar Inyah said in the name of Rav: "The Holy, blessed One has a place and its name is 'secret places'".' The inference can only be that God is the subject of Jeremiah's sentence. But how can one speak of God crying, asks the Talmud in surprise? 'Is there weeping before the Holy, blessed One? For did not Rav Pappa say: "There is no sadness before the Holy, blessed One, as it is said: 'Majesty and beauty are before Him, might and joy in His place' (I Chron. 16.27)?" The Talmud resolves this apparent conflict by noting that 'there is no contradiction here; the one verse applies to the inner, the other to the outer chambers.' In the latter, Rashi explains, there is only joy, but in the former, in the hidden recesses, God weeps.[5]

There have been many times in history, and an infinite number of occasions in the lives of individuals, when people have asked the questions 'What is God doing?' or 'Why isn't God doing something more?' To one who believes in God, but who refuses to, or simply cannot, be blind to the facts of everyday life, such questions are inescapable. What, for example, was God doing during the Holocaust? Rabbi Kalonymus Kalman Shapiro, known as the Piaseczner Rebbe, and later also as the Rebbe of the Warsaw Ghetto, has left us a rare testimony of one who confronted these issues at the time and from within the experience. He suffered in person and he suffered for his people. In the very first days of the war his only son was fatally injured during the German bombardment of Warsaw. While waiting outside the hospital for news of him, his daughter-in-law and his wife's sister were killed by a bomb. Nevertheless, through the bitter months of 1940, 1941 and 1942 the Piaseczner Rebbe continued to lead and encourage his Hasidim, to teach Torah and even to write a book. He worked at this remarkable document until the middle of 1942, when he hid it with the request that, should the author not have survived, it be sent by the finder to the rabbi's brother in Israel. After the war a construction worker discovered the manuscript and the instructions were followed. We thus have a unique testament of creative religious thought written amidst the most terrible depredations.

The following entry, for 14 March 1942, relies on the Talmudic passage just quoted to establish the idea that pain not only needn't prevent God and humanity from finding each other, but can become the very basis on which they meet and hence draw comfort and renewed purpose: 'God, blessed be He, is to be found in His inner chambers weeping, so that one who pushes in and comes close to Him by means of studying Torah, weeps together with God, and studies Torah with Him. Just this makes the difference: the weeping, the pain which a person undergoes by himself, alone, may have the effect of breaking him, of bringing him down, so that he is incapable of doing anything. But the weeping which the person does together with God – that strengthens him. He weeps – and is strengthened; he is broken – but finds courage to study and teach ...'[6] Sorrow which is in itself an isolating thing, undermining religious inspiration, becomes, *in extremis*, the path to partnership.

If communion of this kind is to be sought in times of tragedy and anguish, why should we seek it less in better days when we speak of joy, of wonder and the celebration of beauty. If God suffers in our pain, does God not rejoice in our joy? Surely these are also things we share, grounds on which we meet. As the poet said in the Song of Songs: 'the King has brought me into His chamber; let us be glad and rejoice in You' (1.4). Or, as we say in the wedding blessings: 'Rejoice, indeed rejoice, as your Creator caused you to rejoice in the Garden of Eden of old.' Was God not also happy then, Who fashioned us for this purpose?

3. *To draw close or drive away*

Where there is vulnerability there must also be responsibility. Only the cruel person would seek to exploit the capacity of another to suffer pain. But one who understands that vulnerability is the concomitant of trust, that it has its roots in the readiness to expose oneself to sharing with another for the sake of some task that cannot or should not be undertaken alone, that person seeks to honour and cherish what has been delivered into his or her hands. Thus partnership calls for response. But before we can measure what that response should be, we have to understand the extent of our responsibilities. That in turn depends on an appreciation of the nature of the task for the accomplishment of which God has drawn us into partnership.

Judaism describes the work for the sake of which God chooses to make us partners 'the perfection of the world under the Sovereignty of the Almighty' [the *Alenu* prayer]; that is, the fulfilment of the vision of perfect harmony which prompted God to begin what we now must help complete. Our duty is, as it were, to bring God into the world. We may be no more than tenants here, but it is nevertheless our action which is considered decisive. We may either bring God near or drive God away. The movement of Jewish history, with its dynamic of exile and return, provides a physical paradigm by which either success or failure may be expressed: breach of trust brings exile, honouring trust brings return. In either case the effect is mutual: we go away and drive God away, we come back and God comes with us. This is seen to apply on both the national, indeed the cosmic level, and on the individual plane of each of our lives as we strive to allow God to enter the precincts of our hearts.

In the wider context, the struggle to bring and hold God close is played out upon the stage of history as the building and destruction, the dedication and desecration, of God's house. (This drama is of course metaphorical as well as actual, and so continues to our day.) Thus nothing is more indicative of the return of God's presence to this earth than His entry into the Tabernacle or Temple; nothing so signifies His departure as the sacking of His house. These moments therefore serve to epitomize the manner in which our relationship with God functions and to articulate the nature and extent of our role and responsibilities in it.

The opening section of the Pesikta deRav Kahana explores the implications of the verse (Num. 7.1): 'It came to pass on the day that Moses completed setting up the Tabernacle.' The Midrash uses a play on the word '*kellot*' or 'completed', which it reads also as '*kallat*' or 'bridal', to suggest that the setting-up of the Tabernacle was like the raising of the marriage canopy and the entry of God's presence into it like the entrance of the bride into her bower. God, as it were, comes back down to earth and is united in the closest of bonds with Israel. Return, however, presumes absence; if God comes back, then God must at some previous time have gone away. The Midrash therefore opens by addressing the questions: what caused the Divine Presence to be exiled from the earth in the first place, and what has now brought it back. We read: 'At the beginning of time ... the root of the [divine] Presence was fixed in the regions of the earth below. After Adam sinned, the Presence withdrew to the first heaven.' The generations of Enosh, of the flood, of the dispersion, the Egyptians in the days of Abraham, the Sodomites, the Egyptians in the days of Moses, each caused the Divine Presence to retreat further till it reached the seventh heaven, the utmost limit of its distance from the earth. 'Over against these wicked men, seven righteous men arose and brought it about that the Presence came back to the earth.' Abraham, Isaac, Jacob, Levi, Kohath, Amram, each brought the Presence nearer to the place of its original dwelling. Finally 'Moses arose: The merit he earned brought it about that the Presence came back to the earth.' Hence, on the day he completed setting up the Tabernacle, God's presence entered the bridal bower and was wed again to humankind.[7]

The message of this Midrash, the beauty of which a summary such as this cannot convey, is surely that it is our deeds which determine where God is, whether close or distant, whether near to us or driven far away. Moses' completion of the building of the Tent of Meeting is thus understood as the fulfilment of something much larger, the culmination of a series of reparations whereby God's presence is restored to the place where it was in the beginning. The establishment of the sacred precincts thus both heralds and mirrors the achievement of a greater task, when all the world will be perfected in the great work of redemption and God's presence will fill the whole earth. This, the Midrash implies, will not be achieved by merely 'waiting on the Lord'; just as the creation of the distance between God and humankind is the result of our destructive deeds, so the diminution of that distance can only be occasioned by good actions undertaken by ourselves. For it is in our power to bring God close or to drive Him far away. We are in fact doing one or the other all the time.

Perhaps the most succinct formulation of this principle is to be found in the Ten Commandments, the third of which reads: 'You shall not take the name of the Lord your God in vain' (Exod. 20.7). The significance of this injunction extends far beyond the popular interpretation that it is a prohibition against swearing. To appreciate this one has only to consider the language in which the commandment is phrased. The verb used is *'tissa'*, usually translated as 'take' but literally meaning 'carry'. The negative *'lo tissa'*, 'you shall not take', implies the assumption that we are and should be 'carrying' the name of God; the issue is only the manner in which this is to be done. Indeed, unless we had responsibility for God's name in the first place we could not be required to avoid abusing it by taking it in vain. The real meaning of the commandment is, therefore, that we are answerable for God's reputation and that we must not betray such trust. This is an all-encompassing matter; whatever we do, in particular whatever we do in the name of religion or as people claiming, or considered, to be religious, immediately reflects on God. We have very real power over God's reputation in the world and it is up to us to use it well.

In later Jewish literature this idea is codified as the commandment of *Kiddush Hashem*, by which we are required to sanctify the Divine Name and to avoid its desecration. The biblical basis for this injunction is the verse 'You shall not profane My holy Name and I shall be sanctified in the midst of the children of Israel' (Lev. 22.32). In its extreme form this is taken to mean that we must accept martyrdom rather than deny God or bring His name into disrepute. Indeed, the phrase *Kiddush Hashem* has virtually come to mean dying for God's sake. In fact, though, the principle is much broader, if, mercifully, rather less dramatic. Its implications are co-extensive with life; not a single act or word is irrelevant. Thus each thing well done, in kindness and consideration, with a sense of appreciation and good grace, constitutes a small sanctification of God's name; God's reputation is magnified in the world. The more public the act, the more widespread its consequences, the greater the profile of those who do it, the more God's name is sanctified. In contrast, any act done thoughtlessly, anything which leaves behind it a trail of ugliness, any form of cruelty, diminishes, voids God's reputation. The more public the act, the more widespread its consequences and the greater the reputation of those who do it, the more God's name is desecrated. There is no neutral ground.

When one steps back and reflects on these ideas, when one considers the depth of human responsibility towards God which they imply, one might well feel shocked and startled. Who are we, struggling to manage our short lives as best we can, before the eternal and ever-present being? Why does God permit us to have such influence in His world and how are we to respond to the challenge of using it rightly? The answer, perhaps, is to be sought in the realization that the gift of life, the creation, to use the traditional expression, of the human being with a soul and free will is not only an act of love but an even greater act of trust.

4. *Like the shadow*

Before a child is born, expounds Rabbi Simlai, they teach it the whole Torah and make it take an oath to be righteous and not to be wicked, saying: 'Know that the Holy, blessed One, is pure, His servants are pure and the soul He has given you is pure. If you preserve it in its purity well and good, but if not then know that I shall take it from you.' At the moment of birth an angel strikes the infant on the lip and it forgets all it has learnt. Indeed, on the night of the new arrival's first Shabbat, when it is customary to welcome him or her into the world with words of Torah, one eats the foods of mourning out of sympathy with the young soul's sorrow for the Torah it has lost.[8]

One may, of course, choose to take Rabbi Simlai's words literally, or one may also understand them as an allegory of our life as a whole. We sense, perhaps, that there is something we know, or have once known, a world of purity where the spirit embraced and surrounded us. Unable to perceive this any longer, only rarely experiencing the world like that, we feel that our soul has indeed been taken from us. We long for its return. In prayer, in meditation, through sensitivity to the inner life of people and of all things, we experience its presence once again. Our existence becomes a pattern of searching and losing, a kind of hide and seek with the sense of the spirit, though soon we come to understand that this is no arbitrary game; we ourselves are largely responsible for the conditions which enable us to discover, or which of necessity repel, the presence for which we search. Thus our moral life and our spiritual life are bound one to another.

It is one of the great achievements of Hasidic teaching that it provides us with a language capable of articulating in a direct and accessible manner the dynamics of this personal relationship with God. Such a language emerges from the stress placed by the movement on the importance of the immediate sense of connection between each individual and God and on the fine awareness of the effect of every action on this relationship and hence on the divine vitality itself. One of the most familiar expressions of this dynamic is an interpretation quoted by the early masters in the name of the Ba'al Shem Tov on the phrase 'God is your shadow' from Psalm 121. The idea is that God is as near to every person as his or her own shadow and, like a shadow, mirrors his or her behaviour. Kind actions arouse God's mercy and induce an appreciation of God's closeness; angry deeds awaken the divine wrath and the attribute of judgment, thereby distancing the consciousness of God's protective presence. This, the Ba'al Shem Tov maintained, holds true not only with regard to the overtly 'religious' sphere of our lives; on the contrary, every aspect of our conduct in each and every sphere in which we act has this effect and is immediately relevant to our relationship with God. Thus the Ba'al Shem Tov interprets the famous verse 'You shall love your neighbour as yourself, I am the Lord' in the following remarkable manner: 'As you behave towards your neighbour in companionship and solidarity, as you are, so am I, the Lord. That is, I the Lord shall be like you. This is the secret meaning of "the Lord is your shadow" … Just as a person behaves below towards his friend and companion, so does the most high King behave towards him, in the same way as a shadow which copies every movement of a man.'[9] His construction of the verse, based on a simple relocation of the pause from the customary notation so as to yield 'you shall love your neighbour; as you so am I, the Lord', permits him to emphasize with brilliant simplicity the impact every single human action has upon God. Nothing is neutral, nothing is irrelevant, and no room is left for passivity. There can be no question, in our immediate lives at least, of doing nothing and simply waiting for God. Our relationship with Him is something we are in and part of all the time, whether we know it or not.

In an equally remarkable passage, the later Hasidic leader Rabbi Levi Yitzhak of Berditchev, who studied under the Ba'al Shem Tov's successor, Dov Baer of Mezeritch, elaborates on the relationship between the human being and God using the familiar biblical image of the love of father and son. The sole aim in life of the child who appreciates and reciprocates the love in which his parent holds him is 'to give joy to his Father in heaven, as our sages, may their memory be for a blessing, have said: "Israel nourish their Father in heaven by means of Torah, prayer, faithful action and the keeping of the commandments." But when, alas, the opposite happens [and the child gives pain to its parent] our sages, may their memory be for a blessing, have said: "What does the Shechinah, the Divine Presence, say? She says: My head is hurting me!" It is as if the Creator, blessed be He, were experiencing pain.'[10] This is only one among a number of such physical images that we find in many areas of Jewish literature. No less graphic, for example, is the Talmudic depiction of evil actions performed in secret as 'pushing away the feet of the Divine Presence' (Kiddushin 31a). God is directly, and often painfully, affected by what we do in every act. Indeed, this interpretation vividly articulates the sense of silent but palpable cruelty and violence which is so much a part of contemporary, and perhaps of all, human society.

Of course it has to be remembered that we are speaking in metaphors. Such interpretations as those quoted above, if taken literally, would be anthropomorphic to the point of absurdity. Nevertheless, this kind of language places a particular and powerful focus on the immediacy of our relationship with God. There is not, nor could there possibly be, any denial of the belief that God knows, does and can do all things, or that God's transcendent essence is infinitely beyond our knowledge. But it is something else which is perceived to be most relevant to our spiritual concerns: down here on earth it is not just what God does to us, but equally or more so what we do to God, that matters. God who makes us becomes God who responds to us.

The fate of the world may be determined less by what God makes of us than by what we make of God. For, as we have seen, God, in ever more intimate ways, is described as close to us, following us, mirroring us and, not least, hurt by us. One is reminded of William Blake's famous epigram 'Eternity is in love with the productions of time'. (It was framed, of course, in an entirely different context, though not perhaps without a knowledge of related cabbalistic ideas.) According to the perspective from which we have been looking at the matter, it is the productions of time which control the impact of eternity in the temporal world at least, and God, furthermore, desires it to be that way.

This leads us to the consideration of a further aspect of the teachings quoted above, the premise that we exercise considerable control over the course which our relationship with God may take. In the classic Hasidic phrase, it is the impulse from below that awakes the impulse from above. What this means is that the initiative rests with us; if we want God to respond, we have to take the first steps. It is a strange thought, perhaps, that in our relationship with the all powerful Deity we should be empowered. But it is a power which originates only in humility, which comes, to repeat Shcharansky's phrase, from 'a feeling of submission and respect for God's essence'.[11]

If this is the case then we have a profound responsibility towards God, a duty which we cannot evade, as it is reflected both in our relationships with other people and in our contact with the natural environment around us. For there is no action that is not a response to the trust reposed in us. To the person who perceives all the world as vital, as, in the words of Gerald Manley Hopkins, 'charged with the grandeur of God', life becomes a constant drama of betrayal and respect. Any hurt is deeply damaging, any good profoundly healing and every form and facet of existence responsive to our acts and our intentions. There is nothing, not the smallest item in creation, which does not matter.

The Three Pillars of Judaism

This attitude is well illustrated by the following story which Rabbi Aryeh Levin tells about his first encounter with Rav Kook. The two of them, he recalled, went for a stroll in the fields after Minchah (the afternoon prayer): 'On the way I plucked some branch or flower. Our great master was taken aback; and then he told me gently, "Believe me: In all my days I have taken care never to pluck a blade of grass or flower needlessly, when it had the ability to grow or blossom. You know the teaching of the Sages that there is not a single blade of grass below, here on earth, which does not have a heavenly force (or angel) above telling it, Grow! Every sprout and leaf of grass says something, conveys some meaning. Every stone whispers some inner, hidden message in the silence, every creation utters its song."'[12] Few people have been so imbued with spiritual sensitivity or so mindful of the Divine Presence as Rav Kook, but many have shared the vision of the Prophet Isaiah that at the end of days 'they shall neither hurt nor destroy in all My holy mountain' (11.9). But which will come first, one might well ask, the day when the mountain will be holy or the time when none will hurt or destroy? The answer has surely to be the latter. The mountain is the whole wide world, and the Presence of God will abide there when nothing and no one drives it away. And when, in turn, will that come about? When we are worthy of the trust reposed in us and mindful of the responsibilities that accompany it.

The opposite of this mindfulness is cruelty. Cruelty hurts not only its immediate object but the entire world as well. It inflicts harm not only on victim and perpetrator but even on God, whose faith in us we have abused. Cruelty, therefore, is the epitome of evil. Not only are we forbidden to practise it; we are commanded to strive to mitigate its effects, to nurture its victims and to undo the damage it causes. For cruelty is the greatest barrier to the manifestation of God's presence.

In the end one cannot avoid the word love. It is present, after all, in the Torah's most embracing statement about our relation-

122

ship to God, in which we are commanded to love the Lord our God 'with all our heart, with all our soul and with all our might' (Deut. 6.5). But we return to the word with an appreciation of its mutuality. It is impossible to love without exposing oneself to the impact of another. God, if our relationship with Him is real, will change our lives. But the same is true the other way round. This may not mean that the Infinite Being will be effected in the depths of the remote and hidden concealment, in the Divine separateness which we cannot know, by our response during a brief space of time here on earth. But it does imply that our relationship with God makes a significant, palpable difference to the degree to which God's Presence is manifest here and now in the world.

Such responsibility makes a humbling subject for reflection. In the last verse of the famous hymn *Adon Olam* we say: 'Into His hand I commend my spirit.' This thought and the contemplation of the trust in God required of us if it is to be made real are remarkable indeed. But no less striking is the consideration that at some level, to speak figuratively, God is saying the very same thing to us: 'Into your hands have *I* commended *My* spirit.' We have to appreciate that God has done this despite the fact that our hands are small, unreliable and mortal.

5. God's question

It is often assumed that it is we who ask the questions and God who must give the answers. It is on this basis, for example, that one might arrive at the notion of 'the failure of God': if God makes no reply from heaven, if God fails to intervene at those key moments when every promise, every divine utterance indicates that He should, if God protects neither the innocent nor the weak, then hasn't God failed? The limitation of this approach, which presents enormous, perhaps in our time the greatest of all religious challenges, is that we may not be the only ones who are asking the questions.

There is a well known story about the meeting between the Chief of the Russian Police and the Alter Rebbe, Schneur Zalman of Liadi. Schneur Zalman was accused on false charges and taken off to prison in St Petersburg. There the Chief of Police came to visit him. He immediately realized that he had in his custody no ordinary human being. Something of a scholar himself, the Chief asked the Rebbe what might be the meaning of the verse (in the story of the Garden of Eden) 'The Lord God called to the man and said to him: "Where are you?".' 'Surely,' the Chief commented, 'the Holy, blessed One, knew perfectly well where Adam was!' The Rebbe replied: 'The interpretation of the verse is that God calls out to every human being all the time, saying to him: "Where are you? Where are you in the world?" For a certain number of days and years have been allocated to every person in order that every day and every year he should do what is good before God and towards other people. Therefore reflect: Where are you in your world? How many years of your life have gone by and what have you accomplished in those years?' ...[13] Thus God's first question is God's eternal question, to each and every one of us. We too are addressed by it, not once, but at every instant of our lives. Of course, we do not hear it all the time, but it speaks to us at certain moments, some as unpredictable as sudden bad news, some as regular as the sound of the ram's horn. I know of one rabbi who held his Shofar up on Rosh Hashanah and showed the congregation how it had the shape of a question mark. Each year, each day and each moment God asks us the questions.

It seems to me that the more one becomes engaged in the spiritual quest, the more the balance changes. For sure, issues do not go away; there are questions one has to, one cannot choose but, ask of God. After all, wasn't it Abraham, the father of our faith, who put the challenge for the first time: 'Shall not the Judge of all the earth do justly?' (Gen.18.25), bestowing venerable ancestry upon humankind's oldest and most vexed demand of God? But increasingly such questions as that are balanced, if not superseded, by a consciousness of constant interrogation, the sense that every situation, every person, even every object silently demands of us a conduct befitting its and our existence. It is as if all things, both the animate and even the inanimate world of river and mountain, were calling to us to be more heedful, more mindful of the exigencies and privileges of such encounters. They speak with the lonely voice of a vulnerable spirit, and they speak to us with the voice of great joy. But always they require us to be more worthy of the partnership which their undefined questions imply. It is as if all things were mediators of the Creator's first challenge: 'Where are you?' More and more, we live not only as the ones who ask, but also as the ones who have to answer, answer with our lives.

Nevertheless, there are questions which we cannot choose but ask. If God was the first to put the question 'Where are you?', God has certainly not remained the only one to do so. As much as God asks it of us, we ask it of God. 'Where are you, God?' is the anguished, anxious, hopeful plea of both individual and community in the face of the anticipated blow. 'Where were you, God?' is the pained, angry, helpless demand of relatives, of survivors who pass the eye of the storm where others drowned. It has been said that we ask the wrong questions when disaster befalls and that this is why we are so frustrated. Maybe that is correct. But there are certain kinds of anguish which have to be given a voice. Although it is a truism that there neither is nor can be an answer to the question 'Where was God?', it is inevitable that we should ask it. Being human, caring about our own flesh and blood, we cannot help but do so. We do not need to think of the Holocaust; every case of pointless suffering and injustice anywhere in the world raises the same intractable problems. The challenge can neither be avoided, nor put to rest with a neat, convenient response. A theology which proclaims the Divine justice and the Divine compassion cannot ignore the contrary evidence which human experience has presented since time immemorial. There have been many attempts through

Jewish history to respond to the dilemma of innocent suffering. It has been said that we cannot fathom the ways of God, that God has hidden His face, that we are a sinful generation and have brought our just deserts upon ourselves or that the righteous must suffer for the sake of others. What all these views have in common is that they are valiant attempts to make comprehensible that which lies beyond our understanding. But they are attempts alone; they have value not as answers but as courageous confrontations. They become unacceptable, perverse even, when, as sometimes happens, they are turned into vindictive explanations by heartless know-alls who use them to inculpate others: You sinned, therefore God is punishing you; they sinned, therefore God is punishing them. Such people should be mindful of the Talmudic dictum that the reward of the house of bones is silence.[14] There are things which it is impudent to pretend to understand. One wants to turn, as Job eventually did to his 'comforters', and say: 'Would that you were silent!' And, like Job, shunning facile explanations, we have to return to the question. The answers will change, as answers they scarcely matter. What remains is the question and the need to confront it over and over again: 'Where are you, God?'

But there is still a third question to consider. Anyone who has heard him speak will have taken to heart the words of Rabbi Hugo Gryn, himself a survivor of Auschwitz, that the real issue of the Holocaust is not 'Where was God?' but 'Where was man?' The third question, then, is the one we ask each other. How was it possible for humanity not to have listened? How could the door have been closed on the starving fugitive, the frightened child, the herded parents, the people crammed into the building, the freight car, the oven, the pit? If we fail to ask those questions, how will we ever learn, how will we ever change? If humanity fails to take responsibility for the past, it will be damned in the future to constant repetition of its grossest corruptions.

126

These three questions, God's 'Where are you?' to us, our 'Where are You?' to God, and the mortal 'Where are we for one another?', may at first sight appear to point us in three different directions. Thus the first directs us to reflect upon human nature, the second – in so far as it is possible – on the mysteries of theology, and the third on society and the basis of communal responsibility. But the three questions can also be understood as converging towards a single point. For God's challenge to us can be answered only in the context of our response to one another, and the way we relate to one another depends on our ability to find God's presence in all life and in every place throughout the world. The real issue, therefore, is whether the next steps we take will be away from, or towards, each other. Will we draw closer to one another and to God, will we draw closer to God in a way that helps us to find one another, or will we all go our separate ways, calling out our questions and challenges from an ever increasing distance? We will all be the losers if we do the latter. None of us, not even God as Creator, can exist in isolation. All the questions thus converge into a single challenge: How can we move closer to each other?

Here we are presented with a crucial choice. Is the next step God's responsibility, or ours? Judaism provides us with an unequivocal answer; it has never believed in sitting idly by and waiting for the Lord to do His thing. We must take the initiative. Equally, though, Judaism does not counsel us to place our faith in the unguided actions of human beings. Instead it speaks of partnership. Such partnership is understood to be the basis of creation. This, according to the teaching of Avraham Mordechai of Gur, is the meaning of God's words 'Let us make man'. For God says to each person 'Let us make a human being, I and you together.'[15] Why, then, should God answer our questions, why should God be concerned with how we humans treat one another, if we don't address that issue first ourselves? If we strive to make ourselves and each other into true human beings, God will join us in the task. Response, therefore, has to begin with us. There is sound sense in the saying that 'God helps those who help themselves'. But the principle goes further than the common-sense context in which the adage is generally applied, extending beyond our need of God to include God's need of us. For God, it is suggested, needs us for His sake just as we need God for ours: unless we work on creation together, it will remain incomplete. Therefore God, being committed to its fulfilment, is Himself completed and fulfilled through the perfection of this task. As Chaim Potok said in a recent interview: 'I think the God whose face is turned to us is a God still struggling with the matter of Creation. He or She or It is still in the process of Creation, and we are feeling the imperfection of that process ... I don't think Creation is over.'[16] Having considered God as One who suffers with us, who is vulnerable and dependent, who entrusts His reputation to us, we must conclude by speaking of the God who waits for us to answer His question so that He can answer ours, of God who waits impatiently and who suffers while He waits.

For sure this is only one tiny part of the picture. But, as regards most of the rest, we do not even know how to think about, let alone describe it. God the transcendent, God who fills the infinite spaces of the universe, is beyond the limits of both our language and our thoughts. But, as the Prophets and the Psalmists and Rabbis and poets through the ages have intuited, known and endeavoured to express, God is also closer to human beings 'than their own spirit, their own flesh' (Yehudah Halevi), and waits for us to exercise the responsibilities which such proximity and trust demand.

6. *Upon three things*

Let me return, in conclusion, to the saying which I have taken as the basis for this book. While writing these chapters, especially the last, I have repeatedly been struck by the fact that Shimeon ha-Tzaddik makes no reference to God amongst the three things on which, he teaches, the world depends. This absence is strangely conspicuous. To suggest that it might be an oversight would be absurd. On the contrary, the lack of mention of God must be part of the meaning of what he wishes to convey. What then does it imply?

Perhaps, however, it is wrong to over-emphasize the point. Why, after all, should Shimeon ha-Tzaddik expressly refer to God? None of the three duties of the Jew to which he points would, after all, make any sense at all if there were no God who cared about us and about whom we were obliged to care. Whose Torah is it that we should study and obey? To whom should we be praying and to whom should our actions be faithful, if not to God? Thus the centrality of God need not be mentioned explicitly, because it is so obviously implied.

Nevertheless, it is a striking thought that Shimeon ha-Tzaddik chooses not to say that the world depends directly on God, but rather to state that it stands upon three pillars each of which must be constructed out of human, out of our, endeavour. Clearly, it is this that he wishes to emphasize. He wants those who hear him to understand that the fate of the world lies not in God's but in their, our, very own hands, and that almighty, infinite and unchanging as God may be, God has nevertheless chosen to share with us the responsibility for our joint creation. Though God's presence in it is, of course, vital, it is we who must make that presence actual in mind and heart and deed.

Hence, in speaking of Torah, Simon the Just underlines our obligation to conduct ourselves before God and towards one another in a manner which, rather than driving the Divine Presence away, leaves the world fit to be its abode. Instead of subsisting as a greedy, driven beast, each person has the duty to accept the moral and spiritual disciplines which make us truly human and thus partners with God. In speaking of prayer, Simon the Just stresses the service of God and communication with Him. We do so not only to ask for our immediate needs and those of our people, but to lift ourselves to where we can see beyond the limited bounds of our own existence and perceive and participate in the greater life of which all things are part. By so doing we both strengthen our desire to study Torah and discover the inspiration to conduct ourselves thoughtfully and with courage in the everyday world. Finally Simon the Just requires us to act according to the principle of *Gemilut Hesed*, acts of faithful love, so that what heart and mind come to know may be expressed in ways which make a practical difference in the world. For while it is not in our power to cause the earth to be filled with God's glory, there are doors which only we can open.

Notes

Introduction

1. E. M. Forster, 'What I Believe' (1939), in *Two Cheers for Democracy*, Penguin Books 1972, 75.
2. Talmud Shabbat 31a.

I. Prayer

1. Rabbi Abraham Isaac Ha-Cohen Kook, *Olat Re'iah*, Jerusalem 5759, Introduction, 13.
2. A. J. Heschel, *Quest for God*, Crossroad Publishing Co, New York 1987, 61–2. The quotation comes from E. S. Ames, *Religion*, 217.
3. Ibid., 62.
4. Harold S. Kushner, *When Bad Things Happen to Good People*, Pan Books, London and Sydney 1982, 122.
5. In Lionel Blue and Jonathan Magonet, *The Little Blue Book of Prayer*, Fount Books, London 1993, 23.
6. Kushner, *When Bad Things* (n.4), 125ff.: this is the theme of the chapter 'God Can't Do Everything'.
7. Talmud Berachot 32b.
8. Tosafot there, beginning *Kol Hama'arich*.
9. Zalman Shazar, *Morning Stars*, Philadelphia 1967, 17.
10. Shulchan Aruch, Orach Chayyim 62.2, n.3 in Mishnah Berurah there, and Shulchan Aruch, Orach Chayyim 101.4, n.13 in Mishnah Berurah and Biur Halachah.
11. Talmud Berachot 29b.
12. Yehudah Halevi, *The Kuzari*, 5.5. The translation is taken from Michael Fishbane, 'Prayer', in *Contemporary Jewish Religious Thought*, ed. A. Cohen and P. Mendes-Flohr, Collier-Macmillan, New York and London 1987, 723.

13. The reference is to Hilchot Tefillah 1.2.
14. Rabbi Shalom Noah Brosovsky, *Sefer Netivot Shalom*, Jerusalem 5749, Volume 1, Tefillah Ma'amar Aleph, 182.
15. Ibid.
16. Talmud Berachot 30b, 32b.
17. Shulchan Aruch, Orach Chayyim 101.1, gloss of Moses Isserles there.
18. Talmud, Bava Bathra 164b, Tosafot beginning *Iyyun Tefillah*.
19. Rabbi Nachman of Breslav, Likkutei Moharan 65.2.
20. See n.6 above.
21. Talmud Berachot 5a.

II. Torah

1. A. J. Heschel, *Quest for God*, Crossroad Publishing Co, New York 1987, 105.
2. Mishnah Peah 1.1.
3. Talmut Berachot 5b.
4. Translated from 'Tzva'at HaRibash' ('The Ethical Will of the Ba'al Shem Tov') in *Sefer Shivchei HaBa'al Shem Tov*, Jerusalem 5729, 218.
5. Talmud, Shabbat 31a–b.
6. Maimonides, '*The Book of Knowledge*, Laws of the Foundations of the Torah 2.2', in I. Twersky, *A Maimonides Reader*, Behrman, West Orange NJ 1972, 45.
7. M. Gilbert, *Schcharansky; Hero of Our Time*, Penguin Books 1987, 402.
8. R. Hirsch, *Judaism Eternal,* ed. and trans. I. Grunfeld, London 1956, Vol.2, 216.
9. Quoted in P. Mendes-Flohr and J. Reinharz (ed.), *The Jew in the Modern World – A Documentary History*, Oxford University Press, New York 1980, 163: 'The Reform Rabbinical Conference at Frankfurt – The Question of Messianism'.
10. Yeshayahu Leibowitz, 'Commandments', in *Contemporary Jewish Religious Thought*, ed. A. Cohen and P. Mendes-Flohr, Collier Macmillan, New York and London 1987, 71.
11. Given in the name of Rebbe Menachem Mendel of Kotsk in, for

example, *Pitgamei Hasidim*, ed. Simcha Raz, Jerusalem 1981, 53, and frequently quoted elsewhere.

12. Mishnah Avot 2.5.
13. D. Ellenson, *Rabbi Esriel Hildesheimer and the Creation of a Modern Jewish Orthodoxy*, Alabama 1990, 89.
14. This phrase was taken from the Mishnah (Orlah 3.9) and turned into a popular slogan of nineteenth-century ultra-Orthodoxy. Whereas in the Mishnah the word *hadash* refers specifically to the new cereal crop before the Omer is offered, the technical meaning was dropped and the sentence used to condemn anything new in Judaism.
15. Talmud, Menachot 29b.
16. Following Y. Zevin in *Sippurei Hasidim,* volume on Torah, Jerusalem 5715, 263.
17. In *Shema: Collected Poems of Primo Levi*, trans. R. Feldmann and B. Swann, Menard Press, London 1976, 21.
18. L. Blue and J. Magonet, *How To Get Up When Life Gets You Down*, Fount Books, London 1992, 198.
19. J. Soloveitchik, *The Lonely Man of Faith*, New York 1992, 2, 6–7.

III *Gemilut Hasadim – Acts of Faithful Love*

1. Yehudah Amichai, from Poem no.20 (untitled) in the collection *Hazeman*, Tel-Aviv 1977.
2. Talmud Kiddushin 40b.
3. Mishnah Avot 2.21.
4. Talmud Shabbat 127a.
5. Talmud Succah 49b.
6. Midrash Bereshit Rabbah 49.2.
7. Lore Salzberger-Wittenberg, *Himmel und Erde*, Frankfurt am Main 1966, 41–3 (the translation and summary are my own).
8. Part of one of many conversations I have been privileged to have with the remarkable psychotherapist Dr Lawrence Goldie.
9. Talmud Berachot 5b.
10. Maimonides, Hilchot Mattanot Aniyyim 8.10,11; Talmud Bava Batra 8a–b.
11. Talmud Shabbat 127a.
12. Mishnah Megillah 4.3.

13. Nehama Leibowitz, *Studies in Bereshit*, fourth revised edition, Jerusalem, 185–6.
14. Talmud Sotah 34b.
15. Martin Luther King, 'Letter from Birmingham City Jail', reprinted in *The World Treasury of Modern Religious Thought*, ed. Jaroslav Pelikan, Little, Brown and Co, Boston, Toronto, London 1990, 607.
16. Osip Mandelstam, poem no. 307 in *Selected Poems*, translated by Clarence Brown and W. S. Merwin, London 1973, 78.
17. Mishnah Tanhuma Kedoshim 8. With gratitude to Ismar Schorsch, whose commentary on this midrash I discovered in *The Melton Journal*, New York, Spring 1992.
18. Mishnah Bava Kama 2.6.

IV. *The Hidden God*

1. Thus, see the view of Bet Hillel in Talmud Rosh Hashanah 17a that 'great in loving kindness' (Exod.34.6) means that God inclines towards mercy.
2. Talmud Shabbat 12b.
3. Shemoth Rabbah 2.7, quoted and translated by Nehama Leibowitz in *Studies in Shemot*, Jerusalem 1986, 57.
4. Talmud Berachot 3a and see note in Steinsaltz edition, Israel 1976, 15, beginning *'Nichnasti Lechurbah'*.
5. Talmud Hagigah 5b.
6. Nehemiah Polen, *The Holy Fire, The Teachings of Rabbi Kalonymus Kalman Shapira, The Rebbe of the Warsaw Ghetto*, Jason Aronson Inc., New Jersey and London 1994, 119.
7. Pesikta de-Rab Kahan, trans. W. G. Braude and I. J. Kapstein, Great Britain 1975, 5–6.
8. Talmud Niddah 30b.
9. Sefer Ba'al Shem Tov on Sidrah Kedoshim.
10. Rabbi Levi Yitzhak of Berditchev, *Kedushat Levi*, in his commentary to Sidrah Kedoshim.
11. M. Gilbert, *Schcharansky; Hero of Our Time*, Penguin Books 1987, 402.
12. Simcha Raz, *A Tzaddik in Our Time*, Jerusalem and New York 1977, 108.

Notes

13. Shlomo Yosev Zevin, *Sippurei Hasidim*, volume on Torah, Jerusalem 5715, 12–13.
14. Talmud Berachot 6b.
15. Rabbi Avraham Mordechai of Gur, quoted in Chummash Peninei Hassiut, *Sefer Bereshit*, Jerusalem 5747, 11.
16. Joshua O. Haberman, *The God I Believe In*, The Free Press, New York 1994, 217.